PARTITION AND GENOCIDE
MANIFESTATION OF VIOLENCE IN PUNJAB
1937-1947

Anders Bjørn Hansen

Foreword by Ian Talbot

India Research Press
new delhi

Published by

India Research Press
B-4/22, Safdarjung Enclave, New Delhi – 110 029.
Ph.: 6196234; Fax : 4618637
e-mail : bahrisons@vsnl.com
2002

2002 © India Research Press

ISBN : 81-87943-25-4

Cataloging in Publication Data
Anders Bjørn Hansen
Partition and Genocide : Manifestation of Violence in Punjab 1937-1947
by   Anders Bjørn Hansen

Includes bibliographical references.
1.   Politics.   2. Genocide.   3. South Asia 4. Democracy / Human Rights.
5.   Partition / Divide sub-continent.   6. India / Pakistan.   7. Title.

Printed in India by Focus Impressions, New Delhi – 110 003.

India Research Press
B-4/22, Safdarjung Enclave, New Delhi – 110 029
Ph.: 6196234 Fax : 4618637
e-mail : bahrisons@vsnl.com

Acknowledgements

This present work was embarked upon in 1997 during my stay at a small European University Centre for Peace Studies in Austria. Following a discussion on genocide, where a fellow Pakistani Punjabi student argued that partition violence should by viewed as genocidal, even though it was perpetrated by two sides, I was drawn into the problematic of reciprocal genocide. However, at that time I never would have imagined, that I would spend the next four years, interspersed with some much needed intervals, working on the partition of Punjab from a genocidal perspective.

During the course of my research, I have benefited tremendously from interaction with many scholars. First of all, I wish to thank my supervisor Professor Carl-Axel Gemzell at the Institute of History, University of Copenhagen, for his effort in making clear what I wanted to say. The British Association for South Asian Studies (BASAS) provided me with an opportunity to interact with a number of scholars on South Asia including Pritam Singh, Shinder Thandi and Ishtiaq Ahmad. Special thanks to Professor Ian Talbott for inviting me to Coventry in March 2001 to present my study at the BASAS workshop and providing a number of valuable advice, comments and critique. I must thank Professor Uffe Østergaard and the Danish Centre for Holocaust and Genocide Studies for funding my visit to the BASAS conference. I should also thank Professor Ashis Nandy, Professor Eric Markusen and Shail Mayaram for their valuable comments on my work.

Last, but not least, I wish to thank my wife, Ravinder Kaur, for the tremendous effort she has put into supporting the publication of this present work. This book is truly dedicated to her. However, needless to say any responsibility for omissions or faults are mine alone.

Foreword

Comparatively little has been written about communal violence in the Punjab during the decade which preceded independence. There has been little attempt to understand this period as the pre-history of the partition related massacres and migrations which claimed so many Punjabi victims. In one important respect this lacunae reflects the understanding developed in this book by Anders Bjørn Hansen that the August 1947 violence was qualitatively different to the communal riots of an earlier era. Undoubtedly not only in its extent and level of organisation, but in the invasion of the private sphere in which women were the chief sufferers, there was an added horror in 1947 to what had come before. Moreover, as Anders Bjørn Hansen demonstrates, the violence became uncontrollable not just because of the collapse of the administrative machinery in the wake of partition, but because of the disorder in the Punjab countryside which had previously been relatively tranquil. A final difference was the use of violence to 'ethnically cleanse' minority communities. It should be noted that this had its antecedents in the March 1947 attacks on minority communities in the Rawalpindi division of Punjab. Ethnic cleansing had also lain behind the so-called communal war of succession in Lahore throughout the months preceding the British departure and the publication of the partition boundary award. Nonetheless, it is important, as this work does, to focus not just on the communal violence of 1947, but on the disorders during the preceding decade.

The tensions in such cities as Rawalpindi, Lahore and Amritsar which are clearly brought out in this work, reveal that what happened in August 1947 was not just a 'temporary madness', but was rooted in deep-seated mistrust and bitterness. This work touches on some of the proximate and longer term causes of the sporadic bouts of violence which earned the colonial Punjab the unenviable epithet of the 'Ulster of India.' Trivial events such as the exchange of insults between groups of young men could as easily spark violence, as the playing of music before mosques, the coincidence of festivals in the religious calendar, or disputes over sacred space as in the celebrated Shahidgunj episode in Lahore. Riots not only reflected existing tensions, but also polarised communities. Divisions were further intensified by the mushrooming of volunteer movements during the closing years of British rule. The press also played its part in heightening tensions, sometimes unintentionally, but often unscrupulously.

Hansen reinforces the existing understanding that the countryside, while not immune from conflict, was much less afflicted than the towns. This raises the argument that urban violence could be understood in terms of a transition to modernity, rather than as a result of the playing out of traditional primordial rivalries. Attentive readers can glean from this study that part of the explanation of the tension in

Lahore, for example, stemmed from the growing challenge to the entrenched economic power of the Hindu business class arising from an increasingly prosperous and educated Muslim community. Each town in the Punjab possessed its unique political economy of communalism. This book because of the richness of its sources begins to provide the data for such an analysis.

The work also raises the important issue of the role of politics and community identity in the development of tension and eventual violence. The colonial state was able to structure the Punjab's rural politics around cross-community lines. This ensured that almost to the end of the British era, the main division was between perceived rural and urban economic interests. The Unionist Party institutionalised this political approach and its leading members were able to ensure relative tranquillity in the countryside. The British were prepared to pour considerable economic and political resources into this arrangement to maintain order in the Punjabi countryside which formed the heartland of the Indian Army. It was only when the rural Muslim population finally deserted the Unionist Party that the conditions were created for the bloodletting of 1947.

The colonial state excluded urban politicians from power following the 1937 introduction of provincial autonomy. In contrast to the countryside, economic rivalries in the towns were structured along community lines. The colonial state itself had unwittingly encouraged a sharper drawing of reli gious boundaries as a result of its Census operations, its perceived support for Christian missionary activities and by the granting of separate electorates.

Indigenous religious revivalist movements such as the Arya Samaj thrived in the conditions of urban Punjab. Religious revivalism become increasingly competitive. It became politicised with the introduction of representative institutions. The sense that Punjabi Hindus were a 'dying' community under threat from Christian and Muslim proselytism was reinforced by growing economic competition as a Muslim professional and business class slowly emerged. Sikh religious revivalism had been prompted by the fears of reabsorption into the Hindu fold. Both the Hindu Mahasabha and the Akali Dal were the long term outgrowths of these anxieties. The Muslim urban community also turned to communal representation in the form of the Muslim league.

By the beginning of the 1940s, two distinctive political cultures had emerged in Punjab. In the countryside, cross-community co-operation prevailed, while in the towns, politics were structured around community lines. The Congress was much weaker in Punjab than other provinces of British India. It was identified with the interests of the Hindu urban commercial classes. This marginalised its support amongst the rural Hindu Jat community and prevented it from providing an inclusive nationalist appeal which might have bridged the urban-rural divide.

As Anders Bjørn Hansen reveals, urban communal violence intensified with the onset of the Pakistan movement. This raised similar cultural and economic fears amongst the Hindu and Sikh minorities in the Punjab, to those shared by Muslim minorities elsewhere in India. These anxieties were not only the product of economic and political competition, but of the creation of both neo-Hindu and neo-Sikh identities constructed around the 'myth' of Mughal persecution. Unfortunately, they were to prove self-fulfilling, as increasingly vociferous and eventually violent responses to the Pakistan demand, created the circumstances in which the partition of the Punjab appeared the only solution. Ironically, it was the Sikhs who had the most to lose from the partition of the Punjab who demanded this course of action.

This work hints at the role of politicians from all communities in turning violence to their own purposes. The deadly political embrace of communal conflict was disastrous for the ordinary people of the Punjab. Violence could not be turned on and off like a tap. In the absence of a functioning administrative system, the Juggernaut of communal violence ran out of control in August 1947 with horrific consequences.

The tragedy which is unfolded in this work raises the question could things have turned out differently? The violence in the early years of provincial autonomy was sporadic, rather than endemic. In the normal course of events, millions of Punjabis from different religious communities lived side by side sharing a common language and culture. The colonial state's Fortnightly Reports from which much of the material is drawn here, just as the newspapers, reported only when this normal pattern of living had been disturbed. Especially in the rural areas, co-operation of the various communities was essential for the prosperity of all. One should not read back the tragedy of 1947 to an earlier era and endow it with an air of inevitability. Despite the strictures of the two nation theory, the Muslim, Hindu and Sikh communities were not monolithic. Punjabi society was pluralistic, never monochrome.

Nevertheless, this study reveals that accounts which draw on a rose-tinted view of Punjabi communal harmony cruelly disturbed in the 'madness' of 1947 are as equally simplistic as two nation theory analyses of perpetual community separation. There were deep seated community tensions and mistrust. The strains of economic competition and modernisation were routinely articulated along religious lines. All communities when it suited them could draw on a rich repertoire of symbols and historical events which were inherently divisive. These would have lacked their potency, if communities had intermingled, rather than merely coexisted. It was only in the celebrations of the Sufi shrines that 'distance' was broken down between communities who were otherwise near neighbours, but living in separate worlds.

Anders Bjørn Hansen's work raises many thought provoking questions both regarding the pattern of events in the pre-colonial Punjab and concerning the interplay of state and society in the contemporary subcontinent. It is both an important reference work and an encouragement to think profoundly about the circumstances in which violence can overwhelm community relations. Lessons need to be learnt from the past, if it is not to be tragically repeated in the dangerous world of the opening years of the Twenty First century.

Professor Ian Talbot   October 2001
Coventry

Table of Contents

Introduction

"And I became aware of religious differences. It is sudden.
One day everybody is themselves - and the next day they
are Hindu, Muslim, Sikh, Christian. People shrink, dwindling
into symbols".
Bapsi Sidhwa "Ice-Candy-Man".

Partition of Punjab - Ethnic Cleansing and Genocide

The partition of Punjab in August 1947 constituted a humanitarian catastrophe with an estimated death toll of 500.000.[1] The carnage that swept through the province of Punjab during the summer and fall of 1947 was unprecedented and seemingly unexpected. The partition was accompanied by the largest ethnic cleansing ever recorded in time of peace with more than nine million people crossing borders between the two embryonic states of India and Pakistan. Around 5,4 million Muslims fled from the eastern to the western part of Punjab and 4 million Sikhs and Hindus fled in the opposite direction. On their way to

---

1. There is no consensus on number of casualties and the estimates varies from 200.000 as argued by Penderel Moon: Divide & Quit, Delhi 1998 (first published 1961), to 800.000 as argued by Urvashi Butalia: The other side of Silence. Voices from the Partition of India, New Delhi 1998. G.D. Khosla has argued the number of casualties was 200.000-250.000 on each side. G.D. Khosla: Stern Reckoning: A Survey of the Events Leading Up to and Following the Partition of India, London 1950, (2nd ed., Delhi 1989).

1

presumed safety they were attacked, the men were killed or forcefully converted and women raped, abducted, converted by force or simply killed. No mode of transport appeared to be safe. The marching band of refugees were attacked, the trains were derailed, ransacked and people massacred. The male members of each of the three different religious communities constituting Punjab namely Hindus, Muslims and Sikhs participated in the carnage. For most people it was an inferno of horror and death almost impossible to comprehend.

This study aims to examine the case of Punjab as an example of ethnic cleansing and genocide - and to study some of the mechanisms behind this. It is not aimed at giving a whole explanation of the genocide in Punjab but to point to the genocidal characteristics of the violence.

The importance of this understanding, however, it not only limited to the historical context. Present day politics in South Asia continues to be affected by the aftermath of partition. Furthermore, a study of the manifestation of violence in the Punjab can also enhance our understanding of present day conflicts involving ethnic cleansing and genocidal violence. Particularly in civil-war like situations where two or more communities are fighting for hegemony over given territories or resources. The current understanding of mass violence/ethnic-cleansing/genocides is based on the pre-requisitioned presence of two groups of

2

which one is perpetrator and the other victim. But in a civil-war like situation, as in the Punjab, it is difficult to qualify the given opposing groups in the well-defined categories of victims and perpetrators. Each group is capable of being the perpetrator and the victim depending on their power and influence in given areas. It is in these situations that a new understanding is required that goes beyond the traditional view of genocidal violence.

The Punjab: A Brief Political History

The name, Punjab, derives from the Persian roots wherein *punj* means five and *aab* means water. The five rivers of Punjab- Sutlej, Jhelum, Ravi, Beas and Chenab- earn the region its distinct identity. The historical and undivided Punjab, located in the north-western part of the Indian subcontinent, bordered Afghanistan to the west and the central Indian plateau to the east with the tough mountain terrain of Kashmir to the north and the sandy dunes of Sind and Rajastan to the South.

Historically, Punjab has been a region of turmoil as well as home of great civilisations. The highly evolved Indus valley civilisation flourished here between c. 3000 BC to c. 1500 BC till it gave way to the Vedic society.[2] The Aryan tribesmen were just the first of many invaders that this region

---

2. For a detailed reference on this period read Romilla Thapar, The History of India I, New Delhi, 1987.

attracted at frequent intervals. The most notable among them was Alexander of Macedonia, who in 327 BC marched across Central Asia into Punjab. He was met with utmost resistance from the natural barriers of five rivers, at the last of which his soldiers refused to go any further. The Huns and the Arabs continued raiding the area for a long time, but the real challenge came from Turkish noblemen organised under Mahmud of Ghazni in the late 10th century. Their interest was based on the fabled wealth of the country and especially the fertility of the Punjab plains. The invasions were almost an annual feature conducted around the harvest time to replenish the Ghazni treasury.

Muhammad of Ghauri revived this tradition of frequent raids in the late 12th century and came to be known for his insatiable desire for wealth and iconoclastic activities. Though, he directed his campaigns chiefly against the temple towns famed for their wealth all over northern India, he set his eyes on the richer Punjab plains for establishing the seat of power. Incidentally, the resistance offered against these invasions was extremely disorganised. The Indian historian Romilla Thapar while explaining the defeat of the various Indian principalities mentions firstly, the superior military might of the Afghans aided by the swift Central Asian horses and secondly, and more importantly, the lack of comprehension of the full implications of the invasions in terms of foreign and domestic policy because "the region of Punjab (.) throughout the centuries had been involved in

4

the politics of Afghanistan and Central Asia".[3] This implied a highly volatile politics in Punjab based on a similar Central Asian model, which lent a sense of uncertainty and therefore, a high mobility among the populace.

However, a permanent development at this juncture was the emergence of a Afghan- Turk political entity in the region called the *Delhi Sultanate* or 'the Empire'. The frequent invasions gave way to permanent encampments and Lahore emerged as the centre of Punjab politics. There were frequent palace coups and infighting among the new ruling class and the political chaos prevailed till the arrival of Mughals from Central Asia in 1517. Even though they established a vast empire that extended beyond north Indian plains, the region retained its strong political influence. The Mughals ruled uninterrupted from then on till the British conquest of the Indian subcontinent.

Around the same time a new religion arose as a protest against the Brahmanical domination in the Punjab region. It was part of the *Sufi*[4] movement that attempted a dialogue between Hinduism and Islam. The new religion called *Sikhism*, was monotheistic and tolerant and soon enough it became the people's religion. However in the year 1699 the martial tradition called *Khalsa*[5] was initiated by the

---

3. Ibid.
4. Sufi movement refers to the emergence of the unorthodox spiritual belief in the 15th century India.
5. Khalsa which literally means the pure one, refers to the initiation of the martial tradition in the Sikh religion on the 13 April 1699.

tenth Guru of the Sikhs in response to the growing Mughal domination. The Sikhs underwent a swift radical transformation that turned the sect into a militant community. The crowning glory of the Sikh history, though, was the empire created by Maharajah Ranjit Singh (1784 - 1839) that encompassed Kabul and Kashmir besides the plains of Punjab. The first Sikh kingdom was modern in many ways as it had a highly trained army that employed many European officers, a strong state with a secular outlook. Officers drawn from all the three major communities i.e., Hindus, Muslims and Sikhs, were in change of the state administration.

Though a Sikh nation had been formed successfully in Punjab, it did not translate into a Punjabi nation.[6] That a Punjabi identity had not been evolved was made apparent after Ranjit Singh's death in 1839. The religious identities superseded that of a common Punjabi identity. This was proved later in the gory communal violence during the Punjab partition in 1947.

After a decade long chaos, Punjab was finally annexed by the British in 1849. This also marked the beginning of a long association of the Punjabi's with the British Indian Army. The militant tradition of the Punjabi's and Sikhs in particular was almost given an official certification by the

---

6.   Percival Spear, History of India II, New Delhi, 1978 p 135.

British with its martial race theory. The finest soldiers were believed to be found among the Muslim tribes of Salt ranges, the Sikh Jats and the Hindu Dogras.[7] This loyal relationship between the Punjabi's and the British was manifested during the 1857 revolt as they played an important part in reimposition of the British authority in northern plains. By 1875, the Indian Army drew 1/3 of its soldiers from Punjab that rose to 3/5 in 1914 and by 1945 50% of the soldiers in the Indian Army was Punjabi amounting to a total of one million in its ranks.[8] The British patronage to the Punjabi militant tradition was to play a vital role in the communal violence during the Partition.

Punjab, thus, embarked on road to prosperity and wealth as it was handsomely rewarded by the British for its expression of loyalty. This prosperity, however, resulted in an affluent but still disunited Punjab. The superimposed unity barely hid the smouldering communal passions beneath. To a large extent the economy in Punjab was also divided along communal lines, where the Muslims generally speaking were peasants, while Sikhs and Hindus had more urban vocations too. Thus, while the majority of Muslims were peasants, most moneylenders were Sikhs or Hindus, which fuelled the communal animosity, especially during the later

---

7.   Ian Talbot: "British Rule in the Punjab, 1849-1947: Characteristics and Consequences", Journal of Imperial and Commonwealth History, Vol. XIX No. 2, (1988), London, p 207
8.   Ibid.

part of the nineteenth century where many peasants had to abandon their land since they could not pay their debts.[9] Another cause for communal estrangement between Muslims and Hindus/Sikhs was the movement for cow-protection that developed during the latter part of the nineteenth century as well. It was seen as a way for Hindus to emphasise their 'Hinduness'. The cow-protection movement did, however, create a need among many Muslims to emphasise their 'Muslimness' by exercising what they viewed as their right to kill cows[10], perhaps even more so in a Muslim majority province as Punjab.

According to the 1941 census of India, United Punjab had a population of 28.4 millions. Of these 16.2 millions were Muslims, 7.5 millions Hindus and 3.7 millions were Sikhs (Christians, Parsees etc. constituted the rest). While Muslims mainly lived in the western districts with Hindus predominantly living in the eastern, the Sikhs were mostly situated in the central parts of Punjab.[11] Through out the province, however, all three major communities were present in each of the 29 districts with the central ones being the most diversified. The partition of Punjab totally altered these

9.   Bimal Prasad: Pathway to India's Partition, vol. 1, The Foundations of Muslim Nationalism, Delhi 1999, p. 120.
10. Ibid., p. 219.
11. G. D. Khosla: Stern Reckoning: A Survey of the Events Leading Up To and Following The Partition of India, London 1950, (2nd ed., Delhi 1989), p. 90. In the two eastern divisions Ambala and Jullundur, Muslims constituted 28, per cent and 35 per cent respectively, while in a western division like Rawalpindi the percentage were 85.

characteristics and divided the historical entity of the Punjab into two new provinces in India and Pakistan. In the census of India from 1951, eastern Punjab (in India) was inhabited by 61% Hindus and 35% Sikhs, pointing towards a massive exchange of population.[12]

Previous Research on the Partition of India and Punjab

In Indian historiography the partition of the country has had a problematic position, mainly because it placed a shadow over the long fought struggle for independence. The division of British India into Pakistan and India and the partition of the Punjab and the Bengal provinces based on religious affiliation stood as a testimony over the national movement's inability to unite the country. The partition has therefore been seen as an unfortunate departure from an otherwise glorious road to independence. A focal point in the writings on partition has been the course of Muslim separatism and in this connection the role of Muhammed Ali Jinnah, leader of the All India Muslim League.

The traditionalist school[13] regards the poor election result in the 1937 provincial elections and the controversy

---

12. Quoted in Swarma Aiyar: Violence and the State in the Partition of Punjab 1947-48, London 1994, p. 3.
13. Anita Inder Singh has given the most elaborate account of the traditionalist stand in her: The Origins of the Partition of India, 1936-37, Delhi 1987. See Also R.J: "Jinnah and the Pakistan Demand", Modern Asian Studies (henceforth MAS), 17, 4, 1983, pp. 529-61.

regarding the failure of the Congress and the Muslim League to form a coalition ministry in United Province in 1937 as a crucial turning point for Jinnah making him a religious bigot. The revisionist school, on the other hand, with its main exponent Ayesha Jalal,[14] rejects the thesis of Jinnah turning into a religious fanatic. She perceives him as an excellent real-politician who, in an attempt to avoid political oblivion, only changed his tactics after the election. However, both schools thus view the 1937 election as a major event in the development towards partition and mainly view partition from the All India level of high politics.

The partition has also been approached from a regional point of view. The works of David Gilmartin[15] and Ian Talbot[16] especially created an important shift away from a

---

14. Aeysha Jalal: The Sole Spokesman. Jinnah, the Muslim League and the Demand for Pakistan, Cambridge University Press 1985. Francis Robinson, in a review article in MAS, argued that Jalal's use of newly available material had revealed "the inner coherence" of Jinnah's policy. In the same article, Robinson strongly criticise Stanley Wolpert, associated with the traditionalist school, for not using the new material available in his book: Jinnah of Pakistan, New York 1984. "Aeysha Jalal shows us just how much Wolpert failed to see". Francis Robinson: "Reviews of Stanley Wolpert: Jinnah of Pakistan, New York 1984, & Ayesha Jalal: The Sole Spokesman, Cambridge 1985", MAS, 20, 3 (1986, pp. 611-618. For a debate on the Traditionalist and Revisionist schools see, Asim Roy: "The High Politics of India's Partition. The Revisionist Perspective", MAS, 24, 2, 1990, pp. 385-415.

15. David Gilmartin: The Religious Leadership and the Pakistan Movement in the Punjab, MAS, 13, 3 (1979), pp. 485-517. & David Gilmartin: Empire and Islam. Punjab and the Making of Pakistan, London 1988.

16. Ian Talbot: "The Growth of the Muslim League in the Punjab, 1937-1946", Journal of Commonwealth and Comparative Politics, 20, 1, (1982), p. 5-24, & Ian Talbot: Provincial Politics and the Pakistan Movement: The Growth of the Muslim League in North-West and North-East India 1937-47, Karachi 1988. Ian Talbot: Punjab and the Raj 1849-1947, New Delhi 1988. Ian Talbot: "British Rule in Punjab 1849-1947: Characteristics and Consequences", Journal of Imperial and Commonwealth History, 19, 2, (1991), p. 203-221.

focus on Muslim politics at the All India level to the role played by the Muslim majority provinces, stressing the crucial importance of Punjab in creating a Pakistan: "It formed the heartland of a future Pakistani state, Jinnah indeed called it the 'Cornerstone of Pakistan'. If the Punjabi Muslims had not supported the Muslim League's separatist demand, Pakistan could never have come into existence".[17] However, the pioneering works on regional level began by focusing on Muslim minority provinces like the United Province[18], and it was only at the beginning of the 1980's that Punjab Studies really began to emerge as a separate field in South Asian historiography.[19]

The Indian historian, Bimal Prasad, has recently prepared 'a definitive study of the background of India's Partition'. In this three-volume work, called 'Pathway to India's Partition'[20], he puts forth his thoroughly researched

---

17. Ian Talbot: Provincial Politics and the Pakistan Movement: The Growth of the Muslim League in North-West and North-East India 1937-47, Karachi 1988, pp. 82.

18. Francis Robinson: Separatism Among Indian Muslims: The Politics of the United Provinces Muslims 1880-1923, Cambridge 1974. Paul Brass: Language, Religion and Politics in North India, Cambridge University Press 1974. Following Brass's work an interesting debate occurred in Journal of Commonwealth and Comparative Politics concerning the role of Islam in Muslim separatism.
     Francis Robinson: "Nation Formation: The Brass Thesis and Muslim separatism", Journal of Commonwealth and Comparative Politics, 15, 3 (1977) p. 215-230. Paul Brass: "A Reply to Francis Robinson", Journal of Commonwealth and Comparative Politics, 15, 3 (1977), p. 231-234.

19. Of earlier works Kirpal Singh: Partition of Punjab, Patiala 1972, was one of the first attempts to look at partition only in respect to Punjab.

20. Bimal Prasad: Pathway to India's Partition, vol. 1, The Foundations of Muslim Nationalism, Delhi 1999, vol. 2, A Nation within a Nation, 1877-1937, Delhi 2000. The 3rd vol., The March to Pakistan, 1937-1947 has (unfortunately) not been published at the time of completion of this book.

argument about the primary cause of partition i.e., the strength of Muslim nationalism. He criticises the focus of previous researches that they are based either on the British policy or the various decisions made by the Indian political leaders, between 1937 and 1947. "Neither the League's adoption of the demand for Partition (1940) nor its success in securing fulfilment within a short span of seven years can be explained without reference to the deep historical as well as socio-political foundation of Muslim nationalism, based on a belief that Muslims, although living together with Hindus and others on Indian soil, constituted a nation separate from the rest and had their own special interests to protect and promote".[21] In his view, the folly of most historians has been to regard Muslim nationalism as something that suddenly came about in 1937 (or 1940). Instead, he argues, that Muslim nationalism should be dated back to the later half of the nineteenth century, centred on Muslims institutions such as the National Muhammadan Association in Calcutta and the Muhammadan Anglo-Oriental College at Aligarh, both founded in 1877.[22]

Against the focus on the development at the political level, an attempt has been made to shift the focus and write "history from below" in order to study at the micro level and to focus on marginalised groups. Through the series

---

21. Bimal Prasad, vol. 1, op., cit., p. 11.
22. Ibid.

'Subaltern Studies'[23] and in Gender studies[24] an attempt has been made to write history from this perspective and in this connection to introduce new kinds of sources and approaches. Several recent works have focused more on the victims of the violence than on the violence per se. Gyanendra Pandey emphasises the need for the historian to 'recover the voices of the marginal', so that history does not end up as the celebration 'of certain victorious concepts'. The historian should also move away from the traditional sources and look more towards fictional writings and memoirs, since it would present a medium for otherwise indescribable horrors and sufferings. Pandey criticises the partition historiography for not explicitly trying to describe and comprehend the violence and instead disregard it as irrational.[25] Urvashi Butalia has, in her recent book, The Other Side of Silence,[26] used selective interviews to obtain insight into how the marginalized groups, especially the

23. The series Subaltern Studies was started by Ranajit Guha with the attempt to write the history of the subordinate. The first volume appeared in 1982: Subaltern Studies. Writings on South Asian History and Society, Ranajit Guha (ed.). The now 11 different volumes has had several articles on partition: Shail Mayaram: "Speech, Silence and the Making of Partition Violence in Mewat", Shahid Amin (ed.): Subaltern Studies IX. Writings on South Asian History and society, New Delhi 1997. Gyanendra Pandey; "The Prose of Otherness", David Arnold (ed.): Subaltern Studies VIII. Essays in Honour of Ranajit Guha, New Delhi 1994.
24. Urvashi Butalia: "Community, State and Gender: On Women's Agency during Partition", "Economic and Political Weekly", Vol. XXVIII, no. 17, 24th April 1993. Urvashi Butalia: The Other Side of Silence. Voices From The Partition of India, Delhi 1998. Ritu Menon & Kamla Bhasin: "Recovery, Rupture, Resistance: Indian State and Abduction of Women during Partition", Economic and Political Weekly, Vol. XXVIII, no. 17, 24th April 1993. Ritu Menon & Kamla Bhasin: Borders and Boundaries. Women in India's Partition, Delhi 1998.
25. Gyanendra Pandey, "The Pose of Otherness", pp. 188-221.
26. Urvashi Butalia (1998) op., cit.

women, perceived partition. She questions whether it is important to assess who did what, when the central theme should be to look into the enormity of suffering partition created, and she emphasises the need for shifting the focus to groups otherwise neglected, like women, children and untouchables. Lately, however, as argued by Mushirul Hasan the focus on the political history has been somewhat replaced by "the growing interest in 'history from beneath'...restoring a human dimension to partition".[27] Suvir Kaul has, in an edited volume on partition memories, tried to include various aspects of the study of partition "and of its presence in our lives".[28] As a new approach to partition historiography scholars have also looked at the impact of partition in major South Asian cities[29] with a particular interest on the memories of partition in Lahore and Delhi.[30] A former relief worker in India and Pakistan, Richard Symonds, has produced a very informative and personal eyewitness account on his work in western Punjab (in Pakistan) during October and November 1947.[31]

---

27. Mushirul Hasan: "Prologue", in Mushirul Hasan (ed.): Inventing Boundaries. Gender, Politics and the Partition of India, Oxford University Press New Delhi, 2000, p. 13.
28. Suvir Kaul (ed.): "Introduction", in The Partition of Memory. The Aftermath of the Division of India", New Delhi 2001, p. 20.
29. Tan Tai Yong & Gyanesh Kudaisya: The Aftermath of Partition in South Asia", London 2000.
30. Ahmad Salim (ed.): Lahore 1947, India Research Press New Delhi, 2001. See also V.N. Datta: "Panjabi Refugees and the Urban Development of Greater Delhi", in Mushirul Hasan (ed.): Inventing Boundaries. Gender, Politics and the Partition of India, Oxford University Press New Delhi, 2000, pp. 267-286.
31. Richards Symonds: In the Margins of Independence. A Relief Worker in India and Pakistan, 1942 – 1949, Oxford University Press Karachi, 2001.

The historian Swarma Aiyar has presented another critique of the traditional writing of partition history.[32] While acknowledging the importance of studies conducted on the transformation of regional politics 1936-46, she emphasises that these studies have seldom focused on the violence. All of them make reference to the massacres and mass migration, but the violence as such and the actual moment of partition have been met with "an astonishing silence".[33] The emphasis of her study is on crowd behaviour and crowd violence and on how the violence was organised. The recent work of Ian Talbot is also on crowds and collective action while and the same time trying to address the creation of Pakistan from the perspective of "history from below". Ian Talbot also uses fictional literature to explore both "collective representations" and to introduce a human dimension.[34]

In the newly established periodical, International Journal of Punjab Studies, which focuses on Punjab as a cultural and historical entity, several articles have concentrated entirely on the violence and the breakdown of the social

---

32. Swarna Aiyar: Violence and the State in the Partition of Punjab, 1947-48, Cambridge 1994 & Swarna Aiyar: "August Anarchy: The Partition Massacres in Punjab, 1947", in: D.A. Low & Howard Brasted (eds.): Freedom, Trauma, Continuities. Northern India and Independence, Delhi 1998, pp. 15-38.
33. Swarna Aiyar (1994) op. cit., p. 6.
34. Ian Talbot: Freedom's Cry: The Popular Dimension in the Pakistan Movement and Partition Experience in North-West India, Karachi 1996 & Ian Talbot: "Literature and the Human Drama of the 1947 Partition", in: D.A. Low & Howard Brasted (eds.) op., cit., pp. 39-57.
Studies, 1, 2 (1994), pp. 167-195. Tan Tai Yong: "Sir Cyril Goes to India: Partition, Boundary-Making and Disruptions in the Punjab", International journal of Punjab Studies, 4, 1 (1997) pp. 1-20.

15

and cultural order in the Punjab during the 1947 partition.[35] Mohammad Wasseem has described the migration in connection with the partition of Punjab as "one of the most violent processes of ethnic cleansing in recent history".[36] Ian Copland refers elsewhere to the expulsion of Muslims from the princely states of Alwar and Bharatpur (situated in Rajastan and sharing border with Punjab) as "not just a 'communal' episode, but something arguably for worse, a case of systematic 'ethnic cleansing'".[37] Yunas Samad compares the partition experience with the Rwanda case and the break up of Yugoslavia, i.e. with two recent cases of ethnic cleansing and genocide.[38] Shail Mayaram has described the violence following the partition of India as genocidal, thereby suggesting organisation behind it.[39] However, no attempt has been made to systematically examine the partition violence as a case of genocide.

Genocide: Definitions, Debates and the Punjab Case

The massive forced migration following the partition of the

---

35. Mohammad Wasseem: "Partition, Migration and assimilation: A comparative Study of Pakistani Punjab", International Journal of Punjab Studies, vol. 4, 1, pp. 21-41. & Yunas Samad: "Reflections on Partition: Pakistan Perspective", International Journal of Punjab Studies, vol. 4, 1, pp. 43-61. Tan Tai Yong: "Prelude to Partition: Sikh Responses to the Demand for Pakistan", International journal of Punjab
36. Mohammad Wasseem, op., cit., p. 21.
37. Ian Copland, "The Further Shores of Partition: Ethnic Cleansing in Rajastan 1947", Past and Present, no. 160, August 1998, p. 216.
38. Yunas Samad, op., cit., p. 43.
39. Shail Mayaram op., cit., p. 143.

Punjab can definitely be seen as an example of ethnic cleansing, i.e. the altering of the demographic outlook along the ethnic/religious affiliations. However, whether Punjab qualifies as a case of genocide is a more complicated question.

An understanding of the concepts of 'traditional' and 'genocidal' violence is central to this book. A defining feature of the 'traditional' violence in India is the continuity in social and economic interaction in the post-violence phase, understood as the ability of Hindus, Muslims and Sikhs to continue living together after a riot. In this connection the relative absence of rape is also important. Veena Das and Ashis Nandy have argued that an exchange of violence, as in a feud, is justified from the viewpoint of both the victims and the aggressors, because the feud represents "a pact of violence between social groups".[40] Shail Mayaram has used the term 'consensual' violence to describe the violence associated with the feud. It differs from 'non-consensual' violence which is "grounded in the absence of the consent of the victim".[41] Instead the aggressor has to create another source of legitimation for the violence.

Partition violence, Mayaram argues, was different from the feud normally associated with traditional violence,

---

40. Veena Das and Ashish Nandy, "Violence, Victimhood and the Language of Silence" in Veena Das ed., The Word and the World: Fantasy, Symbol and Record; New Delhi, 1983, pp. 177-90
41. Shail Mayaram op., cit., p. 128.

because "the mutuality of exchange of the feud was rendered obsolete".[42] Instead, it was a case of genocidal violence. This distinction between traditional and genocidal violence is essential in understanding the transformation of violence in the Punjab from 1937 - 1947 and the implicit genocidal features therein. One could argue that the violence in 1937 mainly was a case of consensual violence, since the aim was to reinforce the communal territories among the three communities. However, in 1947 the violence had changed into non-consensual violence and appropriated genocidal features, because the aim of the violence turned into an act of survival.

The term genocide was originally coined by the Polish jurist Raphael Lemkin in 1944 and has its origin in Greek and Latin, where 'genos' means race, people or tribe and 'cide' refers to murder. Lemkin, in the first definition ever, defined genocide as: "The coordinated and planned annihilation of a national, religious or racial group by a variety of actions aimed at undermining the foundations essential to the survival of the group as a group".[43] Lemkin's particular focus on intent was later reiterated in the UN Convention on the Prevention and Punishment of the Crime of Genocide from 9th December 1948, where, in article II, genocide is defined as:

---

42. Ibid, p. 143.
43. Raphael Lemkin: Axis Rule in Occupied Europe, Washington 1944, p. 79.

"In the present Convention, genocides means any of the following acts committed with intent to destroy, in whole or in part, a national, ethnical, racial or religious groups, as such: (a) Killing members of the group, (b) Causing serious bodily or mental harm to members of the group, (c) Deliberately inflicting on the group conditions of life calculated to bring about its physical destruction in whole or in part, (d) Imposing measures intended to prevent births within the group, (e) Forcibly transferring children of the group to another group."[44]

However, the discussion on reaching a concise definition on genocide has nevertheless continued within genocide studies for the last 50 years or so. The majority of genocide scholars have criticized the UN Convention for its omission of other groups than national, ethnic, racial and religious, i.e. the exclusion of political, social, economic and other kind of groups. Thus, many attempts have been made to redefine genocide along with an ongoing debate on the emphasis of intent in the UN Convention.[45] Pieter N. Drost made one of the first attempts to redefine genocide.

---

44. United Nations Convention on the Prevention and Punishment of the Crime of Genocide, 1948.
45. For a critique of the convention, especially on the conventions omission of political groups, see Leo Kuper: Genocide. Its Political Use in the Twentieth Century, Yale University Press 1981 pp. 19-39 and B. Whitaker: Report on the Question of the Prevention and Punishment of the Crime of Genocide, United Nations Economic and Social Council, 1985. For the debate concerning intent; see George J. Andropoulos: "Introdoction: The Calculus of Genocide", in George J. Andreopoulos (ed.): Genocide: Conceptual and Historical Dimensions, University of Pennsylvania Press, 1994.

A jurist himself, Drost found that the limited numbers of groups listed in the Convention would make it less effective in protecting minority groups. Instead it should be extended to protect all kinds of human groups. Drost subsequently defined genocide as, "the deliberate destruction of individual human beings by reason of their membership of any collectivity as such".[46] Thus, Drost maintained the focus on intent in committing genocide by emphasising 'the deliberate destruction'.

However, the focus on legal aspects in defining genocide shifted to the power relation between perpetrator and victim as sociologists ventured into genocide studies and new definitions emerged. Vahakn Dadrian argued that "Genocide is the successful attempt by a dominant group, vested with the formal authority and/or preponderant access to the overall resources of power, to reduce by coercion or lethal violence the number of a minority group whose ultimate extermination is held desirable and useful and whose respective vulnerability is a major factor contributing to the decision for genocide".[47] Dadrian thus, different from the jurists, did not emphasise on intent but rather on the 'successfulness' of the attempt to carry out a genocide. In terms of partition violence one could argue that the dominant group in a given area of Punjab i.e. Muslim or

---

46. Pieter N. Drost: Genocide, Leyden 1959, p. 123-124.
47. Vahakn Dadrian: "A Typology of Genocide", in International Review of Modern Sociology 5, 1975, p. 123.

non-Muslim was capable, through its overall resources of power, "to reduce by coercion or lethal violence" the minority group.

The sociologist Helen Fein has also viewed genocide along the relationship between perpetrator and victim, while maintaining an emphasis on intent. She has defined genocide as: "the calculated murder of a segment or all of a group defined outside the universe of obligation of the perpetrator by a government, elite, staff or crowd representing the perpetrator in response to a crisis or opportunity perceived to be caused by or impeded by the victim".[48] The most significant part of her definition was the concept of victims being 'outside the universe of obligation of the perpetrator'. Thereby the perpetrator both as an individual and as part of a collective was exonerated from his action. In the eyes of his own community he would even be regarded as someone executing a moral necessity, while engaging in genocide for the sake of the community or the state.

Helen Fein later made a new definition of genocide which was closer to the UN Convention: "Genocide is a series of purposeful actions by a perpetrator(s) to destroy a collectivity through mass or selective murders of group

---

48. Helen Fein"Scenarios of Genocide: Models of Genocide and Critical responses"; in I.W. Charny (ed.) 1984, Toward the Understanding and Prevention of Genocide: Proceedings of the International Conference on the Holocaust and Genocide, Boulder/ London, 1984, p. 4-5.

members and suppressing the biological and social reproduction of the collectivity. This can be accomplished through the imposed proscription or restriction of reproduction of group members, increasing infant mortality, and breaking the linkage between reproduction and socialization of children in the family or group of origin. The perpetrator may represent the state of the victim, another state or another collectivity".[49] By focussing on purposeful actions Fein emphasised the importance of intent with a sociological bias.

The debate on definition has thus been the most central and structural discussion within genocide studies.[50] Its prominence should be seen in the struggle between, on one hand, wanting to make the Convention more operational in order to prosecute perpetrators and, on the other hand, the ambition to obtain a sociological comprehension of the concept of genocide. While there is no clear consensus on definition, there is, however, an understanding of the pivotal role of the state in perpetrating genocide. The first scholar to emphasise upon the role the state was Irving Louis Horowitz. He argued that: "Genocide is a structural and systematic destruction of innocent people by a state bureaucratic apparatus".[51]

---

49. Helen Fein: Genocide - A Sociological Perspective, 1993, p. 24
50. I have looked into this problematic elsewhere. See Anders Bjørn Hansen: "Folkemordsforskningen gennem 50 år – En definitorisk tilgang" in: Den Jyske Historiker, nr. 90 (Folkemord), december 2000, pp. 39-59.
51. Irving Louis Horowitz: State, Power and Mass Murder, 1976.

Two of the most prominent scholars Frank Chalk and Kurt Jonassohn have defined genocide as "a form of one-sided killing in which a state or other authority intends to destroy a group, as that group and membership of it are defined by the perpetrator".[52] However, by emphasising on 'one-sided killing' they exclude victims of civil war, for e.g., in principle cases like Rwanda and Bosnia. The partition violence further challenges such definitions since there was no singular perpetrator or victim group. The killings were engineered and executed by all three religious communities in their spheres/localities of influence. The historian Mark Levene has similarly argued "that the perpetrators of genocide are states, or state-sanctioned bodies",[53] even though he recognises that such an exclusive approach creates several problems especially to present day cases of mass killings. In the acts of genocide committed both in Bosnia and Rwanda in 1990's, it is not possible to identify the state as the single uniform perpetrator.[54] Furthermore, there is nothing in the UN Convention which suggests that genocide is a state perpetrated crime only, since it is clearly stated in article IV that "Persons committing

---

52. Frank Chalk and Kurt Jonassohn: The History and Sociology of Genocide. Analyses and Case Studies, Yale University Press 1990.

53. Mark Levene: "Is the Holocaust Simply Another Example of Genocide?", Patterns of Prejudice, vol. 28, no. 2, 1994, p. 4.

54. Mark Levene (1994) op., cit., p. 5, footnote 10. Levene argues that in principle genocide did not happen in Rwanda and Bosnia, "because the apparatus of state - and hence an overwhelming control of the means of systematic violence - has been fragmented between more than one competing group".

genocide or any of the other acts enumerated in article III[55] shall be punished, whether they are constitutionally responsible rulers, public officials or private individuals".

However, as argued convincingly by R.J. Rummel, states and governments have played a major role in the mass murders of the twentieth century. According to his estimates close to 170 million people died between 1900 and 1987 as a result of government sanctioned violations. In order to analyse and compare the magnitude of government perpetrated deaths, Rummel invented a new concept; Democide: "The murder of any person or people by a government, including genocide, politicide and mass killing".[56] Though most genocides have been perpetrated by states, one needs to recognise that genocides are committed without state involvement as well. This is borne by the developments in 1947 during the partition of Punjab. –

In an article on partition literature, Jason Francisco argues that "partition stands as the archetype of ...nationalist fratricide" where people of "common cultural heritage" are competing for "political control of land and government".[57] Francisco, however, differentiates between 'nationalist

---

55. Article III of the convention stipulates that the following acts shall be punishable: "a) genocide, b) conspiracy to commit genocide, c) direct and public incitement to commit genocide, d) attempt to commit genocide, e) complicity in genocide".
56. R.J.: Rummel: Death by Government, New Brunswick, 1994, p. 31.
57. Jason Francisco: "In the Heat of Fratricide. The literature of India's Partition Burning Freshly", in Mushirul Hasan (ed.): Inventing Boundaries. Gender, Politics and the Partition of India, Oxford University Press New Delhi, 2000, p. 372.

fratricide', and what he argues is the "other principle type of ethnic conflict, nationalist genocide,...characterized by State-sponsored persecution or slaughter of cultural or religious minorities".[58] But as argued above, state involvement need not be a pre-condition for genocide and while emphatically arguing that partition violence was a case of killing amongst brothers, Francisco overlooks the significant features on how the violence was organised. (In this regard the interesting point is to understand how the religious identity managed to replace the regional identity, and how the violence was organised and manifested, rather than emphasising a politically motivated distinction between fratricide and genocide). Furthermore, from a sociological point of view, killing among people of 'common cultural heritage' can also be seen as genocidal. And from a legal point of view, religious groups are one of the few mentioned for protection in the genocide convention.

In the Punjab case, neither a state nor a government perpetrated partition violence, but one could argue that the two embryonic states of India and Pakistan were present as a national discourse in the mindset of the people. The exclusiveness of the national discourse became one of the prime motivators during the violence. Very few genocide scholars have looked into partition as a case of genocide because of the lack of state involvement. Genocide scholars

---

58.   Ibid.

Leo Kuper and Leonard B. Glick are both hesitant in describing partition violence as an act of genocide because of the lack of state involvement. Kuper emphasises that this was not a "centrally organised government directed type of genocide" but a case of mob violence. Still he points out that the attacks on selected targets like refugee trains and hospitals did portray a somewhat organised effort.[59] However, according to him, partition violence was constituted by genocidal massacres characterised by "the annihilation of a section of a group - men, women and children, as for example in the wiping out of whole villages".[60] Glick also refers to the violence during the partition of India as a "near-genocidal ethnic-religious conflict", where "the intentions of the combatants clearly qualify as genocidal".[61]

Genocide is a concept with very powerful connotations and should therefore be used with caution. Leo Kuper made a pioneering attempt in 1981 to look at genocide from a comparative perspective. In his book "Genocide. Its Political Use in the Twentieth Century" Kuper argues the difficulty, on one hand, in a rational manner studying brutality, while, on the other maintaining the proper empathy for each victim, not reducing his or her suffering

59.   Kuper op. cit., p. 66.
60.   Ibid., p. 10.
61.   Leonard B. Glick: "Religion and Genocide", in Israel Charny: The Widening Circle of Genocide, 1994, pp. 54-55.

to statistics. He further argues another "preliminary problem in the choice of cases for inclusion. [Since] it involves a judgement that the case is in fact one of genocide. Inevitably this is somewhat personal, and sometimes controversial judgement since there is no international criminal court to investigate charges of genocide, and the United Nations evades the issue".[62] In order to avoid confusion Kuper only included genocides according to the UN Convention. He also refrained from redefining genocide. However, being critical of the omission of political and economic groups, Kuper decided to include them, as well as conflicts where genocidal massacres had taken place. These cases of "non Convention" genocides were named 'Related atrocities' in order to make their inclusion less controversial. Whether Kuper succeeded in his efforts to broaden the understanding of genocide is debatable. If his point was that a given violation of a political or economic group was an act of genocide, then that would be the case whether a politically motivated UN Convention acknowledges it or not. The same should be the case with conflicts where genocidal massacres took place.

Henry R. Huttenbach is one of the few scholars who have argued that genocide is not necessarily committed or executed by states or governments only, since well-armed and well-organised communal group could, given a situation

---

62 Kuper op. cit., p. 9.

with a weak central Government, carry out a genocide. Huttenbach argues that "elements within society, harbouring genocidal intentions, can, with or without the collusion or cooperation of the instruments of the state, embark on a genocide campaign. Under the circumstances of a political disequilibrium, civil strife can erupt generating genocidal forces, one or both sides determined to eliminate the other".[63] Partition violence in Punjab was exactly a case where a civil strife turned into a genocidal conflict where the two sides were aiming at eliminating the other. Furthermore, Huttenbach defines genocide in a very inclusive manner: "Genocide is any act that puts the very existence of a group into jeopardy".[64] However, by using such an inclusive definition it becomes rather difficult to differentiate between genocidal violence and other acts of violence. The psychologist Israel Charny belong to a similar 'inclusivist' position within genocide studies. Charny argues that "whenever large numbers of unarmed human beings" die at the hands of their fellow men, then, "we are talking about genocide".[65] He defines genocide as "the wanton murder of human beings on the basis of any identity whatsoever they share national, ethnic, racial, religious, political, geographical, ideological".[66]

---

63. Henry R. Huttenbach: Locating the Holocaust on the Genocide Spectrum: Towards a Methodology of definition and Categorization", Holocaust and Genocide Studies, vol. 3, no. 3 (1988), p. 296.
64. Ibid., p. 297.
65. Israel Charny: "Towards a Generic Definition of Genocide" in George J. Andreopoulos (ed.): Genocide: Conceptual and Historical Dimensions, University of Pennsylvania Press, 1994, p. 74.
66. Israel Charny (ed.): Genocide. A Critical Bibliographic Review, London 1988.

Several sociologists have tried to understand genocide in a structural context while emphasising that genocide is basically a modern phenomenon and a result of modernity. The sociologists Isodor Wallimann and Michael Dobkowski regard genocide as a phenomenon resulting from "structural violence and the anonymous forces that dominate modern man".[67] According to Zygmunt Bauman the holocaust (and genocides) was a terrible but nonetheless legitimate product of our modern civilisation, where the annihilation (of the Jews) was executed by the rational state. There was no intent, only bureaucratic facilitation.[68] Partition of Punjab can also be seen as the result of a modern project aiming to establish two new nation-states. The "old" multi-ethnic discourse of co-existence amongst Hindus, Muslims and Sikhs was challenged by a "new" national discourse that finally prevailed and became a driving force for the violence.

The UN Convention, and the underlining of intent, has to a large extent witnessed a revival with the establishment of the war tribunals for the former Yugoslavia and Rwanda respectively. For the first time the UN Convention on the Prevention and Punishment of the Crime of Genocide has been put to use. It is now possible to study the jurisprudence from the war tribunals, especially the several convictions of

---

67. Michael Dobkowski & Isodor Wallimann (eds.): Genocide and the Modern Age, New York 1987, p. xvii-xviii.
68. Zygmunt Bauman: Modernity and the Holocaust, Oxford 1989.

genocide from the Rwanda tribunal.[69] There is nevertheless still a need for a comprehensive sociological/ historical definition of genocide that will enable scholars to look deeper into the complicated and diversified processes that leads to genocide in order to, not only understand historical cases of genocides, but also aim at preventing genocide in the future.

Political Power Struggle and Communalism

One of the main characteristics of genocide studies is the dominant role of the study of holocaust. Thus, the majority of research has focused on the annihilation of Jews. In recent years, though, more emphasis has been placed on the comparative approach rather than on the uniqueness of the particular cases. Henry Huttenbach has in the first issue of Journal of Genocide Research thus argued that holocaust and genocide studies should develop into an integrated discipline just called genocide studies. Huttenbach points out that "as knowledge of other genocides expands, the argument seeking to insulate the Holocaust from findings about other genocides, especially those after Auschwitz, no longer persuade. Investigations into recent genocidal massacres growing out of ethnic conflicts uncover categories

---

69.   For a discussion of the importance of the jurisprudence from the war tribunals see: Eric Markusen: "What is Genocide? A Search for Answers" in Steven L. B. Jensen (ed.): Genocide. Cases, Comparisons and Contemporary Debates, forthcoming 2002.

of experience and analytical problems not encountered in the study of the Holocaust".[70]

Thus, the jurist Barbara Harff has (together with Ted Gurr) deliberately used 1945 as a starting point in order to embark on a comparative approach to genocide studies.[71] She has listed three necessary pre-conditions for genocide. 1) Structural change - understood as national upheaval, 2) sharp internal cleavages - combined with historical struggle and 3) lack of external constraints - no international sanctions or intervention.[72] Genocide scholar Robert Melson has also stressed upon similar pre-conditions for genocide and especially argued, that genocides take place when state and society are in crisis, i.e. facing an internal strife.[73]

These three pre-conditions were all amply present in the Punjab case. Firstly, the process of de-colonisation and the creation of the two new states of India and Pakistan

---

70. Henry R. Huttenbach: "Introduction", Journal of Genocide Research vol. 1, 1999, p. 7.
71. Barbara Harff & Ted Robert Gurr: "Towards Emperical Theory of Genocides and Politicides: Identification and Measurement of Cases since 1945", International Studies Quarterly, 1988 32, p. 360.
72. Barbara Harff: "The Etiology of Genocides", in Isidor Wallimann & Michael N. Dobkowski (eds.): Genocide and the Modern Age. Etiology and Case Studies of Mass Death, New York 1987, p. 43. Helen Fein has, while analysis the work of Barbara Harff and Ted Robert Gurr, argued that sanctions against the perpetrator states, so genocide no longer appear as a 'rational way' of erasing a societal problem, is the most likely way to stop potential genocides. Helen Fein: "Accounting for Genocide after 1945: Theories and some Findings", International Journal on Group Rights, 1, 1993.
73. Robert Melson: Revolution and Genocide. The Origins of the Armenian Genocide and the Holocaust, 1992, pp. 15-17.

threw Punjab into a state of complete turmoil. Secondly, the communal differences and the ensuing hostilities constituted the internal strife that was given a historical hue by the political leadership and thirdly, the imminent withdrawal of the British made them extremely reluctant to take up the responsibility of checking the violence. This led to a breakdown of the law and order situation and provided suitable conditions for the conflict to grow unhindered. Thus, the Punjab case fulfils these necessary, though insufficient explanations. This insufficiency necessitates search for other possible explanations, too.

Mark Levene has argued that the emergence of nationalism, especially in multiethnic societies creates what he has named 'zones of genocide' where conflicting national aspirations battle over the same recourses and territory.[74] Thus, it is the transformation of the traditional order or the battle against this transformation which is decisive in creating a 'zone of genocide'. "What is clear, however, is that zones of genocide are created when traditional, multi-ethnic societies are subject to outside pressure in a way that impede and ultimately cancel out paths of pluralist accommodation".[75] With the emergence of at least two competing national discourses in Punjab (Pakistani and

74. Mark Levene: "Creating a Modern "Zone of Genocide": The Impact of Nation and State Formation on Eastern Anatolia, 1878-1923", Holocaust and Genocide Studies, vol. 12 no. 3, 1998, p. 418-419.
75. Ibid.

Indian) the traditional co-existence of the three communities came increasingly under pressure thus creating the pre-conditions for a zone of genocide. However, the Punjab case cannot only be understood in the context of competing nationalisms. Instead we should also look into the notion of communalism as an explanation to the partition violence in the Punjab.

The term communalism denotes a phenomenon where religious affiliation is considered more important than other affiliations. As communalism develops different religious communities in the same locality find it increasingly difficult to coexist. Communalism is based on the construction of 'self' and 'other' and often leads to believe that the 'other' needs to be expelled or terminated from the locality. Even though communalism often has been identified as religious nationalism it is not possible to juxtapose the two concepts. Nationalism and communalism are not necessarily overlapping identities.

The origin of the concept of communalism is still widely debated. Gyanendra Pandey argues that it generated from the British writings on Indian society. The conflict between different religious groups was seen as a typical feature of the Indian society and signified the uncivilised behaviour of the native people. Within the colonial discourse the cause of violence lay in the religious celebrations. The colonial state presented itself as a "wise and neutral power, ruling almost without a physical presence by the sheer force of its

33

moral authority".[76] According to Pandey, communalism was constructed by the colonial state to legitimise colonial rule and reproduced by the colonial archives through what he has termed 'the master narrative'.

Bipan Chandra sees communalism more as a result of colonial rule than as a (conscious) colonial construction. Through their ability to 'divide and rule' the British succeeded in dividing the Indian society.[77] According to Chandra communalism is expressed through various phases beginning with a liberal phase where people belonging to different (religious) groups are still capable of living together, and ending with an extreme phase where the society is overpowered by a fascist ideology, breeding on fear and hatred between 'us and them'.[78] What Chandra has labelled extreme communalism is almost identical with the definition of communalism provided by Pandey: "In its common Indian usage the word 'communalism' refers to a condition of suspicion, fear and hostility between members of different religious communities".[79]

76. Gyanendra Pandey: "The Colonial Construction of 'Communalism': British Writing on Banaras in the Nineteenth Century", Ranajit Guha (ed.): Subaltern Studies VI. Writings on South Asian History and Society, New Delhi 1989, p. 156.
77. Bipan Chandra: Communalism in Modern India, Delhi 1984.
78. Bipan Chandra (1988) op., cit., pp. 398-442. For a further debate on communalism see: K. N. Panikkar, (ed.): Communalism in India: History, Politics and Culture, Delhi 1991. Ayesha Jalal: "Exploding Communalism: The Politics of Muslim Identity in South Asia", in Sugata Bose & Ayesha Jalal (eds.): Nationalism, Democracy & Development. State and Politics in India, Delhi 1998 pp. 76-103. Ayesha Jalal: "Secularism, Subalterns and the Stigma of 'Communalism': Partition Historiography revisited", MAS, 3o, 3 (1996) p. 681-689.
79. Gyanendra Pandey: The Construction of Communalism in Colonial North India, Delhi 1990, p. 6.

In a more virulent form communalism is expressed through the communal riot. The history of the communal riot is generated mainly from the colonial discourse that tends to present the rioting as a uniform event. However, notwithstanding the fact that many riots have a common modus operandi, rioting is far from a uniform or singular phenomenon.

Several studies have been conducted concerning the imperative of politics in the course of collective violence[80] and on the role of crowd.[81] In the study of communal violence the role of crowd has generated an increased interest. The emphasis has been on the set-up of the crowd, whether it was ruled by emotion or by reason and on how the crowds were mobilised.[82] In a comprehensive study on communal violence in Bengal 1905-1947, Suranjan Das shows how the communal violence changed during this period and especially how it was influenced by organised politics.[83] From 1920's onwards the number of recorded riots increased as the general political mobilisation in the

80. David Snyder & Charles Tilly: "Hardship and Collective Violence in France 1830 - 1960", American Sociological Review, 1972.
81. E. P. Thompson "The Moral Economy of the English Crowd in Eighteen Century," Past and Present, 50 (1971), George Rudé: The Crowd in History: A Study of Popular Disturbances in France and England, 1730-1848, New York 1964. However, more recent studies have changed the focus to outside Europe, Ian Talbot: "The Role of the Crowd", Journal of Imperial and Commonwealth History, vol. 21, 2 (1993), Sandria Freitag: Collective action and Community: Public Arenas and the emergence of Communalism in North India, California 1989.
82. Ian Talbot: Freedoms Cry, op., cit.
83. Suranjan Das: Communal Violence in Bengal, 1905-1947",. Delhi 1991.

country began to take form. Mahatma Gandhi's first campaign of civil disobedience in 1920 changed the political discourse in India and slowly involved the masses. In the beginning it was possible for the nationalistic Congress party to unite the Hindus and Muslims during the non-cooperation movement and the Khilafat issue in the early 1920's, but after the campaign was called off following the Chaura Chauri incident in February 1922, Muslims-Hindu unity on a massive scale never happened again. It has been argued, that Muslims felt alienated by the way Hindu religious symbols were used by Congress to appeal to the masses.[84] The break-up of the Khilafat/non-cooperation movement was followed by severe communal backlashes regarding issues such as cow killing and music played in front of mosques at prayer time.[85] In 1923 there were riots reported in Amritsar, Multan and Panipat in the Punjab as well as several other places throughout northern India. "During the five-year period between 1923 and 1927, in all about 450 persons lost their lives and 5,000 persons were injured as a result of communal riots".[86] However, these figures are compiled from the whole of India. The worst riot in India (prior to the period of 1937- 1947 addressed in the work), was in Kanpur in United Province in March 1931, during the heydays of the civil disobedience movement. The rioting, which, continued for three days, resulted in an estimated

84.   Bimal Prasad, vol. 1, op., cit., p. 41.
85.   Bimal Prasad, vol. 2, op., cit., p. 186.
86.   Ibid., p. 186.

death-toll between 400 and 500, while as many as 500 buildings had been either destroyed or damaged.[87]

Thus, during the late 1920's the struggle for political power had further intensified and several references to the need of partition was made in the Punjabi press, even though the idea had a very limited backing. However, in 1933 a Punjabi student at Cambridge, Chaudhury Rahmat Ali, made a demand for the creation of a separate Muslim state, called Pakistan. The demand was subsequently sent to the ongoing session of the Round Table Conference on India.[88] The Conference, however, did not take Ali's demand seriously and disregarded it "as merely a student's scheme".[89] Nevertheless, the concept of 'Pakistan' had been born and that too only a few years before provincial autonomy was achieved in 1937. The communal award from 1932, which was a continuation of separate electorates, had formed the basis for the 1935 Government of India Act, which subsequently led to the provincial elections in the winter of 1936/37. Thus, from 1937 communalism began making an even stronger headway into institutional politics, a development that, according to Suranjan Das, changed the shape of communal rioting in the twentieth century.[90] During the 1940's, i.e. after this change, the religious and communal identity began to prevail. Other feelings of

---

87. Ibid., p. 261.
88. Bimal Prasad, vol. 1, op., cit., pp. 187-189.
89. Ibid., p. 32.
90. Suranjan Das, op., cit., p. 11. Even though Das study is focused on Bengal, his observations remain relevant for the Punjab case as well.

belonging like friendships began subsiding as it became increasingly more difficult to avoid being identified as a Hindu, Sikh or Muslim. The ascribed or born-with identity of religious affiliation prevailed and questioned other ways of belonging. Achieved identities based on friendship or political beliefs were increasingly under attack. Thus, Das emphasises the importance of the political change in 1937 for the further development of communalism and in particular the connection between political power struggle and communalism in South Asia. However, Das has primarily worked on the development in Bengal while the connection between political power struggle and communalism has not been examined in same detail in the case of Punjab.

About this Study: Sources and Methods

In this study the introduction of provincial autonomy in 1937 has been used as a point of departure. The communal violence in India has been the object of much research[91] but the rioting prior to and during the partition in 1947 has not been vigorously studied. This book, therefore, covers the period of 1937-1947, which has previously been studied mainly for the political development leading to partition,

---

91. To mention a few books. Veena Das (ed.): Mirrors of Violence: Communities, Riots and Survivors in South Asia, New Delhi 1990, Sudhir Kakar: The Colour of Violence, Delhi 1996, Asghar Ali Engineer: Communalism and communal Violence in India. An Analytical approach to the Hindu-Muslim Conflict, Delhi 1991. Sandria Freitag, op., cit.

rather than focusing on the different manifestations of the violence. I have attempted to reconstruct and analyse the development of communal violence during this period. The focus of the study is more on the changes in violence during the period than on the partition violence per se.

The study purports to (a) examine the connection between the political power struggle and the development of communalism in the Punjab, (b) examine how the communal violence developed and the changes that occurred in it and, (c) examine whether the communal violence was organised.

This study is mainly built on primary sources, which I collected at India Office Library and Records, London during a stay in February 1998 and supplemented with material found during my study at Jawaharlal Nehru University, New Delhi from 1998-1999. The most important sources are the Fortnightly Reports from the Chief Secretary for the Government of Punjab to the Viceroy (from January 1937 to August 1947) and the letters from the Punjab Governor to the Viceroy.[92] The Chief Secretaries during this period were Indians but the views they expressed were similar to those of the British Governors, which indicates a close interaction between them. The fortnightly reports were

---

92. I have looked at all reports available, written between January 1937 and August 1947, approx. 270 and also included Governor's letters whenever they dealt specifically with the communal situation. See L/P&J/5/238-250, IOL.

constructed around various themes like (a) Political/ Communal relations (b) Crime (c) Press (d) General. Later the 'War' emerged as a separate item and from the end of 1944 'volunteer organisations & private armies' was described as separate items as well.

The fortnightly reports and the Governor's correspondence portray the Colonial Government's information about and perception of the violence in Punjab. These sources are certainly not free of lacunae mainly because (a) the reported incidents are limited to the violent exchanges and (b) it is only the recorded violence which managed to reach the historian in terms of statistics pertaining to people killed, injured and wounded. The sufferings of the victim have gone unnoticed, as argued by Gyanendra Pandey.[93] Moreover, Pandey has argued the problem of evidence when looking at violence, since "large-scale violence destroys much of its most direct evidence".[94] Finally, what the British described as a communal incident might have represented something altogether different for the people involved. There are many examples of the British deliberately describing clashes as incidents of communal violence in order to portray themselves as "just" rulers

---

93. Gyanendra Pandey (1994) op., cit.
94. Ibid., p. 190.

destined to establish law and order.[95] However, the fortnighly reports are the nearest we can come to the events and most importantly the material offers a continuous coverage of the period 1937-47.

To supplement this material I have primarily used two published source collections. The very elaborate 12 volumes work: Constitutional Relations Between Britain and India: The Transfer of Power (TOP) 1942-47 edited by Nicholas Mansergh and Penderel Moon.[96] This collection contains a varied account of the correspondence among the different key persons, both within India but also between the Indian administration and the British Cabinet. To describe the violence that erupted during the partition, I have particularly used a selection of documents compiled by Kirpal Singh, Partition of Punjab 1947.[97] This collection consists of the correspondence and reports compiled among officials in East and West Punjab.

Among the secondary literature, I have made extensive use of British and Indian works on partition located primarily at the Nehru Memorial Museum and Library, New Delhi,

---

95. Gyanendra Pandey: "The Colonial Construction of 'Communalism': British Writing on Banaras in the Nineteenth Century", Ranajit Guha (ed.): Subaltern Studies VI. Writings on South Asian History and Society, New Delhi 1989.
96. Nicholas Mansergh and Penderel Moon (eds.): Constitutional Relations Between Britain and India: The Transfer of Power (TOP) 1942-47, 12 volumes, London 1970-1983.
97. Kirpal Singh (ed.): Select Documents on Partition of Punjab 1947, National Bookshop, Delhi, 1991.

mainly to provide a description of the wider political development. I have also used secondary published material from Pakistan, though it was not frequently available at the library due to the tense relationship between India and Pakistan.

This book is divided into three parts preceded by the Introduction. The first part covers the development from the 1937 provincial elections till the British announcement of their withdrawal in end February 1947. The focus is on the political power struggle and on communalism. The second part deals with the internecine strife among the Hindus, Sikhs and Muslims and covers the period from March 1947 till the transfer of power and independence on 15th August. The third part covers the partition with focus on the violence that followed it, and on how the violence should be defined and explained. The final part consists of conclusions, where I have attempted to see the results in a wider perspective as a case of ethnic cleansing and genocide. Each chapter is structured in a chronological order in an attempt to trace the development of communal violence and is followed by a summary.

PART I

POLITICAL POWER STRUGGLE
AND COMMUNALISM

Chapter 1
First Escalation

From the 1937 Provincial Elections to the Cripps Mission 1942

The Government of India Act of 1935, which was implemented in 1937, gave to a large extent self-government at the provincial level. It furthermore extended the franchise to almost 35 million people in all of India.[98] The 1935 Act, which replaced the 1919 Government of India Act, not only extended the franchise but also opened up for responsible governments i.e. with ministers responsible to legislative assemblies at the provincial level.[99] It also abolished the old system of dyarchy.[100] Thus, the Act opened up for a wider participation in the political process, while at the same time broadened the political power struggle. The Act aimed at giving regional leaders a further say at the provincial level, while securing British superiority at the centre.[101] It, however, neither offered Dominion status to India nor changed the political composition at the centre and was

98. Ayesha Jalal, op., cit., p. 15.
99. Sumit Sarkar: Modern India, 1885-1947, Delhi 1983, p. 336
100. Dyarchy, which was introduced in the 1919 Act, meant that only a limited numbers of portfolios were transferred to the provincial Governments.
101. For an account of the British policy in India during the thirties see D.A. Low: Britain and Indian Nationalism. The Imprint of Ambiguity 1929-1942, Cambridge 1997.

therefore received with much suspicion and criticism by both the Indian National Congress and the Muslim League.

Even though inherent lacunae in the Act were apparent, both the Congress and the Muslim League decided to contest the provincial elections.[102] In the elections, the Congress emerged as the most important party at the All India level, and thus, it considered itself the legitimate and the only challenger to the British Raj. The Muslim League harvested a meagre result and saw their claim as the only Muslim party strongly gnashed by the electorate.

In the Muslim majority province of Punjab, the clear winner in the election was the Unionist Party, a regional party mainly consisting of landowners. It was also an inter-communal party representing both Muslims, Hindus and Sikhs, even though a majority of the party members were Muslims.[103] While the Unionist emerged victorious with a simple majority in the assembly, the Muslim League was completely routed having won only one seat.[104]

The new Government was formed under the premiership of Sir Sikander Hyat Khan from the Unionist

---

102. Anita Inder Singh, op., cit., p. 2.
103. For a description of the Unionist Party see: Iftikhar H. Malik: "Identity Formation and Muslim Party Politics in the Punjab, 1897-1936: A Retrospective Analysis", in MAS, 29, 2 (1995), p. 293-323. Ian Talbot: Khizr Tiwana: The Punjab Unionist Party and Partition of India, London 1996.
104. Ayesha Jalal, op., cit., footnote 67, p. 32. The Congress won 18 seats, including five for the Congress Socialist.

Party. He chose a well-balanced cabinet consisting of three Muslims, two Hindus and one Sikh.[105] From the British point of view, the aim of the 1935 Government of India Act had been achieved in Punjab with the election of a strong pro-British Government with representation of each of the three major communities in the province. However, this also marked the beginning of intense communal politics in the subcontinent that severely affected the communal relations.

Irrespective of the results, the polling for the 1937 provincial election was reported to be peaceful, except in Amritsar where a Hindu nationalist had been fatally injured in a scuffle with some Congress supporters.[106] Even though this incident testified to an intra-community disagreement, by far the most conflicts were among people belonging to different communities. The religious processions, among others, were the most common basis for triggering off a riot. On 27th March a clash took place in Panipat between Hindus and Muslims, where the latter tried to prevent a religious procession from taking place. The ensuing violence killed seven Muslims and one Hindu while leaving twelve injured.[107] The Governor of Punjab, Sir Herbert Emerson, later described the incident as a very bad affair and expressed his fear of communalism.[108]

---

105. Ibid., pp. 22-23.
106. Fortnightly Report (FR) second half of January 1937, in S.A.I. Tirmizi: The Paradoxes of Partition, vol. 1, New Delhi 1998, pp. 111-113.
107. FR second half of March 1937, IOL, L/P&J/5/238, p. 272.
108. Governor's letter to the Viceroy, 24th April 1937, IOL, L/P&J/5/238, p. 264.

In the beginning of May, the overall communal situation was reported to have normalised, but at Kot Fateh Khan in western Punjab tension was acute and there were daily incidents.[109] According to Governor Emerson, the Muslim leadership's feelings towards the Congress were hardening. He explained this with the Congress 'Muslim mass contact campaign' and the "arrogance" of Jawaharlal Nehru.[110] The Punjab Premier, Sikander Hyat Khan warned that: "Congress arrogance is increasing the apprehensions among Muslims of Hindu domination, and communal feelings will soon reach a dangerous level".[111] Jinnah and the Muslim League were strongly antagonised by the campaign and viewed it as an attempt to divide the Muslims and break the League. However, Muslim feelings towards the Congress and its campaign were far from uniform and throughout India several Muslim groups supported the campaign, like the Ahrars in Punjab. Mushirul Hasan has argued that in 1937/38 a common political identity among Punjabi Muslims had yet to crystallise.[112] However, a stronger political awareness had entered the Punjab that steadily changed the nature of conflict among the three religious communities. From being centred around traditional or religious differences per se, the conflict now evolved around the distribution of power,

---

109. FR first half of May 1937, IOL, L/P&J/5/238, p. 236.
110. Jawaharlal Nehru was one of the most influential Congress leaders and in 1937 President of the Congress Party.
111. Governor's situation report dated 22nd May 1937, IOL, L/P&J/5/238, p. 217.
112. Mushirul Hasan: "The Muslim Mass Contacts Campaign: Analysis of a Strategy of Political Mobilization", in Mushirul Hasan (1993) op., cit., pp. 142-143.

though the religious symbols continued to be at the conflictual pivot. [113]

The conflict over religious procession routes remained one of the key reasons for the recurring violence.[114] On 13th June 1937, a major clash took place between Muslims and Sikhs at Kot Fateh Khan because of a Sikh procession. Two or three Sikhs were killed and several injured.[115] The police called out to protect the Sikhs opened fire three times killing five Muslims and injuring many.[116] Symptomatic of the growing inter-communal hostility in western Punjab, there were reports of incidents where Sikhs had been killed. Thus, the overall communal situation was described as deteriorating.[117] The tense relationship between Muslims and Sikhs continued throughout the summer with each community blaming the Government and each other for the rioting.[118]

It seemed that the provincial Government could not easily master the conflicts. On the contrary, the communalist groups were breaking new grounds. The communal rhetoric was appearing with more frequency in the Press and a worried Government had to beg them not to publish,

113. Ibid., p. 150.
114. FR second half of May 1937, IOL, L/P&J/5/238.
115. Governor's situation report dated 19th June, IOL, L/P&J/5/238, p. 199-200.
116. In the following report dated 3rd July it was clarified that the police fired six times. It is also mentioned that all policemen were Muslims.
117. FR first half of June 1937, IOL, L/P&J/5/238, p. 158.
118. FR first half of July 1937, IOL, L/P&J/5/238, p. 145.

"matters calculated to exacerbate communal bitterness".[119]
However, the appeal seemingly had little effect because the
communal violence was appearing at altogether new places.
The violence that had gripped the western Punjab
increasingly spilled into eastern Punjab as well. At the
beginning of September, in Mandi Baha-ud-Din in the
eastern Punjab, a Muslim went amok and wounded two Sikhs
and three Hindus with a sword besides leaving one Sikh
killed.[120] At Sanghi in the Rohtak district, later in the month,
a party of about two hundred Hindu Jats attacked a mosque
because the Muslims had carried out some renovation on
it.[121] During this incident one was killed and five wounded.
The Rohtak district continued to be an affected area in the
latter part of 1937 with several clashes occurring in
connection with Hindu processions, too.

In October, a significant political agreement was reached
between Sikander Hayat Khan and Jinnah called the
'Sikander-Jinnah pact'. According to this new
understanding, all Muslim members of the Unionist Party
were advised by Sir Sikander to join the Muslim League.[122]
One may question the political wisdom of Sir Sikandar for
agreeing to a pact that appeared to benefit Jinnah at a time
when he and the Muslim League were close to political

---

119. FR first half of August 1937, IOL, L/P&J/5/238, p. 118.
120. FR first half of September 1937, IOL, L/P&J/5/238, p. 96.
121. FR second half of September 1937, IOL, L/P&J/5/238, p. 76.
122. Ian Talbot: Punjab and the Raj, 1988, p. 124.

oblivion. But in essence the pact benefited both the parties. Sir Sikander could control the only Muslim opposition to the Unionist Party in Punjab by encouraging his followers to join the Muslim League. He insisted and ensured that the All Indian Muslim League would have no say in Punjabi affairs.[123] Having only limited interest in politics at the centre Sikander did not mind allowing Jinnah to speak on behalf of Punjabi Muslims at the all India Level. However, this concession was essential for Jinnah in his aspiration to make the League a symbol of Muslim unity.[124] The news of the Sikander-Jinnah pact created anger among Sikhs and Hindus supporting the Congress in the Punjab region. They regarded it as a direct Muslim attempt to oppose the Congress. Among Muslims, however, the general feeling was in favour of the pact. The fortnightly report supposed that the agreement would, on one hand result in greater solidarity within each of the three communities and also between Hindus and Sikhs and, on the other hand, "a clearer demarcation within all three communities of the forces hostile to and favourable to the Congress".[125]

During the winter of 1937 and early spring of 1938 there were no reports of any clashes. However, in the beginning of April, trouble broke out in the Jhelum district in the north-western Punjab, where Hindus allegedly had

---

123 Aeysha Jalal, op., cit., p. 39.
124. David Gilmartin op., cit., p. 174.
125. FR second half of October 1937, IOL, L/P&J/5/238, p. 45.

tried to disturb peace. According to the fortnightly report, there had been a certain amount of organisation behind this outbreak and it was supposed that there had been outside instigation as well. Such outside interference was also pointed out in connection with troubles in the villages of Raja Jang and Mir Muhammad in the Lahore district. [126]

Notwithstanding these incidents, by the end of June 1938, the communal situation had improved so much that it was no longer considered necessary to forbid large assemblies of people. [127] The much needed improvement in the communal relationship was maintained throughout the summer and early fall. The fortnightly reports from July to September either did not have communal relations as a special item or described the communal situation as being satisfactory. However, this short lived truce only succeed in giving a much needed respite to the populace, for in the beginning of October, clashes between Hindus and Muslims erupted in the Multan district once again leaving two persons dead. [128] Nevertheless, Punjab ended the year on a peaceful note. In the fortnightly report from the first half of December 1938, it was concluded that, "the communal situation as a whole has been satisfactory". [129] Sir Sikander wrote to Jawaharlal Nehru that it was important neither to magnify nor to minimise the communal incidents that were happening

126. FR first half of April 1938, IOL, L/P&J/5/239, p. 76.
127. FR second half of June 1938, IOL, L/P&J/5/240, p. 168.
128. FR first half of October 1938, IOL, L/P&J/5/240, p. 82.
129. FR first half of December 1938, IOL, L/P&J/5/240, p. 32.

in India. He also assured Nehru that he would do what he could to bring down the level of tension. "Indeed, as you may be aware, it has been and still is my greatest mission in life to bring about harmony and goodwill between the various communities in this great country".[130]

The new year of 1939 brought along sporadic violence, mainly in connection with cases of cow slaughtering. On 28th January, three Muslims and one Hindu were killed at Ratera in the Hissar district.[131] On 2nd March, Muslims tried to interfere with a Sikh procession and in the following clash, one Muslim was killed and seventeen were wounded including four Sikhs and two Hindus. One of the Hindus later succumbed to his fatal injuries.[132] At the end of March it was reported that tension was growing between Ahrars and other Muslim groups as well. Ahrars were being accused of being too supportive of the Congress and during a clash on 21st March one person was fatally wounded.[133]

On the political front there were discussions about changing the representation of the different communities in the municipal services. A proposal giving the Muslims 49%, Hindus 41% and Sikhs 10%[134] against the previous

130. Letter from Sikander to Nehru, 14th February 1939, in Tirmizi op. cit., p. 616.
131. FR second half of January 1939, IOL, L/P&J/5/241, p. 118.
132. FR first half of March 1939, IOL, L/P&J/5/241, p. 78. The report also mentioned tension between Sunni and Shia Muslims.
133. FR second half of March 1939, IOL, L/P&J/5/241
134. FR first half of May 1939, IOL, L/P&J/5/241, p. 27.

40-40-20 was suspended at the end of May in the interest of the Sikh community.[135] The discussions were concluded with a resolution on 10th July, giving 48% to Muslims, 37% to Hindus and 15% to Sikhs[136], in a meeting from which Hindus and Sikhs had walked out. Though this presented a very potent opportunity for triggering off communal violence, the tension was contained.

On 3rd September 1939, in accordance with the 1935 Government of India Act, Viceroy Linlithgow declared war on Germany.[137] At the political centre the British decision was met with a demand for political concessions if the Congress should back the war effort. Nehru, the Congress expert on international affairs, sidelined Gandhi, who initially had declared that India should support the British unconditionally.[138] Instead the British faced a Congress demand for "a post-war constituent assembly to determine the political structure of a free India" and the formation of a "responsible Government" at the centre.[139] Their demands were strongly rejected by the Viceroy.

On 14th September the Congress Working Committee further responded by declaring that India could not participate in a democratic freedom struggle when that same

---

135. FR second half of May 1939, IOL, L/P&J/5/241, p. 13.
136. FR first half of July 1939, IOL, L/P&J/5/242, p. 151.
137. Ayesha Jalal, op., cit., p. 47.
138. D. A. Low (1997), op., cit., p. 298.
139. Sumit Sarkar, op., cit., p. 375.

freedom was denied to her.[140] The Viceroy, having been left in the cold by the Congress, then turned to the Muslim League. On 17th October he announced that Dominion status would be granted in a distant future and promised that post-war consultations would be held with "representatives of the several communities".[141] This announcement challenged the Congress in its claim of representing All India and emphasised that a future transfer of power would not (necessarily) be given to the Congress alone. Instead he de facto allowed the Muslim League a veto on future constitutional changes and Jinnah had come a huge step forward in being the sole spokesman for India's Muslims. However, the Muslim League decided not to back the war effort.

Since March 1939 no communal disturbances had been reported and the outbreak of the World War did not affect the communal relations in the province either.[142] The British perception of the attitude in Punjab and its constituent communities vis-à-vis the war was positive. The Governor expected the different Punjabi communities to support the war effort as "the martial races look forward to recruitment on a large scale".[143] The debacle at the political centre did not have much impact in the Punjab where the Unionist

140. D. A. Low (1997), op., cit., p. 299.
141. Sumit Sarkar, op., cit., p. 376.
142. FR for the first half of November 1939, IOL, L/P&J/5/242, p. 34.
143. FR first half of September 1939, IOL, L/P&J/5/242, p.90

Government supported the war effort. It was the Governor's assessment that even if the Congress and the Muslim League did not back the war effort, the majority of Punjab's Muslims were in support of England.[144]

At the national political level, however, the trouble brewed once again. Because of the rejection of their political demand the Congress announced that they would resign from all parliamentary work on 22nd December. The announcement also included the resignation of the Premiers in all of the seven Congress ruled provinces. Jinnah subsequently labelled it as the 'Day of Deliverance'. In a statement made on 6th December he said. "I wish the Mussalmans all over India to observe Friday, the 22nd December as the 'Day of Deliverance' and thanks giving as a mark of relief that the Congress regime has at last ceased to function".[145] D. A. Low has argued that Jinnah thereby succeeded in making Congress rule equal to Hindu dominance and "swept back to prominence on a wave of sustained hostility towards the Congress".[146]

However, the political turmoil at the centre did not have any immediate impact in the Punjab. After the collective resignations, the various Governors in the Congress ruled provinces assumed office according to section 93 of the

---

144. FR second half of September 1939, IOL, L/P&J/5/242, p.77. Note that nothing is mentioned about the communal relations.
145. Jinnah's statement, 6th December 1939, in S.A.I. Tirmizi: op., cit., pp.868-869.
146. D. A. Low (1997), op., cit., p. 314.

1935 Act. However, the provincial Governments in the Muslim majority provinces Punjab, Bengal and Sindh continued to hold office.[147] The Congress Party was weak in the Punjab and Unionist Party, as mentioned earlier, controlled the Muslim League in Punjab.

In January 1940 it was reported that the disagreement between Hindus, Muslims and Sikhs concerning their representation in the municipal services and procession routes continued to cause tension among them.[148] A more disturbing aspect of these developments was that even the personal relationships, which hitherto maintained a distinction between personal and political, were now affected by the political disagreements. For example, in February a Muslim killed his Hindu friend because he had insulted Islam.[149]

On 19th March a major clash erupted between hundreds of members of the Khaksars, a Muslim volunteer organisation formed among Punjab's Muslims in 1931, and the police in Lahore. During the clash 32 Khaksars were killed and as many as 56 injured. Though the police casualties were far less, two officers died and twelve were injured.[150] In this situation, Jinnah's famous appeal had a dramatic effect. At a Muslim League meeting in Lahore on 22nd March 1940,

147. Ibid.
148. FR first half of January 1940, IOL, L/P&J/5/243, p. 280.
149. FR first half of February 1940, IOL, L/P&J/5/243, p. 251.
150. FR second half of March 1940, IOL, L/P&J/5/243, p. 214-217.

Jinnah officially denounced a common Indian Nation. "It is extremely difficult to appreciate why our Hindu friends fail to understand the real nature of Islam and Hinduism. They are not religions in the strict sense of the word, but are, in fact, different and distinct social orders. It is a dream that the Hindus and Muslims would ever evolve a common nationality, and this misconception of one Indian nation has gone far beyond limits".[151] Jinnah then continued emphasising how Hindus and Muslims belonged to two different civilisations. "To yoke together two such nations under a single state, one as a numerical minority and the other as a majority, must lead to growing discontent and the final destruction of any fabric that may be built up for the government of such a state. Muslim India cannot accept any constitution which must necessarily result in a Hindu majority government".[152] After thus having declared his discontent with what he saw as the kind of democracy for India envisioned by the Congress Party, Jinnah then continued demanding a separate homeland for Muslims. "Musalmans are not a minority, as it is commonly known and understood. One has only got to look around. Even today, according to the British map of India, four out of eleven provinces, where more or less the Muslims dominate, are functioning notwithstanding the decision by the Hindu Congress high command to non-cooperate and prepare for

---

151. Presidential Address of M. A. Jinnah-Lahore, March 1940, in H.D. Sharma (ed.): 100 Best Pre-Independence Speeches, 1870-1947", New Delhi 1998, p. 302.
152. Ibid.

58

civil disobedience. The Musalsmans are a nation according to any definition of a nation, and they must have their homelands, their territory and their state".[153] The next day (23rd March) the All India Muslim League passed the following resolution demanding "that the areas in which the Muslims are numerically in a majority, as in the north-western and eastern zones of India, should be grouped to constitute independent states in which the constituent units shall be autonomous and sovereign".[154]

Within the Traditionalist and Revisionist schools it is disputed as to how the Lahore resolution (later known as the Pakistan resolution) should be interpreted. The traditionalists view the resolution and the two-nation theory as an attempt to establish a separate Muslim state and regard the subsequent independent Pakistan as the logical consequence of the Lahore resolution. The revisionists, however, argue that the Lahore resolution should not be seen as a demand for an independent state, but rather as a bargaining counter. Jinnah wanted that the Muslims in India should be regarded as a nation and not as a minority. His real aim was neither a division of British India nor a partition, but a relationship of equals.[155]

However, disregarding whether the Lahore resolution was meant as a bargaining counter or not, it indeed

---

153. Ibid, p. 303.
154. Ibid.
155. Asim Roy, op., cit.

questioned the idea of a united and multicultural Punjab with a common identity, and thus affected the communal relations. Even though suggestions for some kind of loose federation for the Muslim majority areas had been voiced before[156] and the term 'Pakistan' was already presented by Rahmat Ali back in 1933, it was, nevertheless, the first time the coexistence of Hindus, Muslims and Sikh was so openly denounced as an illusion, and by such a prominent leader too. That Punjab was witnessing a growing communal unrest as was evident already in the beginning of April. During a clash between Hindu Jats[157] and Muslims on 7th at Lehlara in the Rohtak district between 40 and 50 people were injured.[158] And, from the beginning of June it was reported that the different communal and political groups had started organising or reviving their volunteer corps. The Sikhs had their *Jathas* (local defenders) and the Hindus the Rashtriya Swayamsevak Sangh (RSS).[159] While the Jathas were locally organised and independent, the RSS, which was founded in 1925, had branches in several places in North-India. The Hindus were especially anxious because

---

156. Anita Inder Singh, op., cit., p. 56.
157. Jats are a separate group or tribe belonging mostly to North India and especially the Punjab. Jats do not have a homogeneous religious affiliation, hence there are Sikh, Hindu and Muslim Jats. As a group Jats has traditionally been a martial community.
158. FR first half of April 1940, IOL, L/P&J/5/243, p. 202.
159. The RSS was formed in 1925 with the aim of restoring the wounded Hindu pride by constructing a strong Hindu nation. The volunteers were trained in both physical and moral education drawn from the ancient Hindu scriptures. For further reference on ideology and organisational structure read M. S. Golwarkar: We, or our Nationhood Defined, Delhi1939. Tapan Basu, et. al, Khakhi Shorts and Saffron Flags, Delhi 1993 and Christophe Jaffrelot: The Hindu Nationalist Movement and Indian Politics : 1925 to the 1990's, Penguin Books India 1999.

of the growing agitation by the Khaksars, while the Muslims were equally afraid of the preparations made by Sikhs to resist the Khaksar or any other Muslim organisation.[160]

Even though the fall of France in June 1940 caused anxiety in the fortnightly report, the biggest worry for the British was the extreme mistrust between Sikhs and Muslims. Each community was suspecting the other of making preparations for war and the Sikhs publicly condemned a separate Pakistan. Now for the first time the Lahore Resolution was mentioned under the item communal relations. The Sikhs and Hindus in the Punjab perceived the resolution as an attempt by the Muslims to establish Muslim dominance in the province.[161]

The fear of Pakistan expressed by the Sikhs though, was considered to be genuine. The communal clashes in Sargodha and Gujranwala in the central Punjab, on 7th and 13th July respectively, further convinced the Sikhs that they were right in their assumption. The Sikhs were preparing to buy and produce 'kirpans' (swords) as never before.[162] However, in the latter part of 1940 there was no reference to the communal situation at all. In this critical situation, the main concern for British was that even though people

---

160. FR first half of June 1940, IOL, L/P&J/5/243, p. 149.
161. FR second half of June 1940, IOL, L/P&J/5/243, p. 140.
162. FR first half of July 1940, IOL, L/P&J/5/243, p. 126.

in the cities and towns recognised Britain's need for help to win the war, they nevertheless remained unmoved towards doing anything by themselves.[163] Another worry was the possibility of a political alliance between the Akali Sikhs and the Congress, which would strengthen the nationalists.[164]

In February 1941 it was reported that problems with processions continued and that the All India population census in late February was used to strengthen the communal identity. "All three communities have been concentrating on instructing their co-religionists how to register their religion and language in the census".[165] Both the Hindus and the Muslims accused each other of wanting to establish a Muslim or Hindu Raj respectively.[166] Perhaps in an attempt to preserve the communal peace, Sikander Khan, declared on 11th March 1941 in a speech at the assembly, "that he was opposed to a Pakistan which would mean Muslim Raj here and Hindu Raj elsewhere".[167] He argued instead in favour of a loose confederation. On 7th May, nevertheless, the communal peace was rocked once again when riots took place at Bhiwani in the Hissar district southeast of the Punjab leaving nine Muslims dead and injuring 26. Among Hindus two were killed and 15 were injured.[168]

163. FR second half of October 1940, IOL, L/P&J/5/243, p. 32.
164. FR first half of December 1940, IOL, L/P&J/5/243, p. 18.
165. FR second half of February 1941, IOL, L/P&J/5/244, p. 193.
166. FR first half of March 1941, IOL, L/P&J/5/244, p. 173.
167. Sumit Sarkar, op., cit., p. 380.
168. FR first half of May 1941, IOL, L/P&J/5/244, p. 100.

Even though the entry of Soviet Union into the war on 22nd June 1941 was noted with relief, the communal tension continued causing concern. The Hindus were moving closer to Sikhs "for mutual help" against the potential Muslim aggression.[169] At the same time Jinnah was challenging Sikander Khan. In June 1941 Sikander was invited by the Viceroy to serve on the National Defence Council, an invitation which he had accepted. Unfortunately the Viceroy had invited Sikander and other provincial Premiers as representatives of the Muslim community and not as Premiers.[170] This mistake made it possible for Jinnah to force Sikander to resign from the Council, because, according to Jinnah, Muslim League was the sole representative of Muslims. Sir Sikander was forced to accept this position, thereby ending all ambiguity about who was representing the Muslim community at the center.

While Jinnah slowly strengthened his political position at the centre, the war continued to develop at a fast pace. The fast advances by the German troops against Soviet Union in July created fear among the Indian people of getting directly involved in the war.[171] The communal situation, however, remained unchanged. Muslim students had started

---

169. FR second half of June 1941, IOL, L/P&J/5/244, p. 77. (It is also mentioned, however, how Hindus had "expressed resentment" against a Sikh conference where thousands of Hindus were converted to Sikhism).
170. Anita Inder Singh, op., cit., p. 67.
171. FR second half of July 1941, IOL, L/P&J/5/244, p. 60.

a campaign of 'P' for a separate Pakistan.[172] By November 1941 the Sikh opposition to the idea of a separate Pakistan was becoming more outspoken and at the many *Diwan's*[173], during the annual *Nankana Sahib* Fair, speakers were insistent that any attempt to introduce Pakistan would be resisted by force.[174] On the whole in Punjab there was a continuous and growing debate about a separate Pakistan.[175]

The American involvement in the war in December 1941 was reflected with relief in the fortnightly report. Even though there was a firm believe that the Allies would win the war, the report expressed concern over the loss of naval bases due to the Japanese attack on Burma.[176] The first report from 1942 was more concerned with the course of the war, especially the defence of Singapore than with the communal relations.[177] As the war came closer and closer to India, the British found the need to win over the public opinion. The fall of Singapore in mid February was received as a shock and made the public aware of the possibility that India could face an attack.[178]

At the same time the British war cabinet was facing a

---

172. FR second half of September 1941, IOL, L/P&J/5/244, p. 37. (The fortnightly report for the first half of September 1941 was one of the few I found missing in the file).
173. Large religious assemblies of Sikhs
174. FR first half of November 1941, IOL, L/P&J/5/244, p. 21.
175. FR first half of December 1941, IOL, L/P&J/5/244, p. 6.
176. Ibid.
177. FR first half of January 1942, IOL, L/P&J/5/245, p. 133.
178. FR second half of February 1942, IOL, L/P&J/5/245, p. 115.

growing demand from both liberal and conservative groups in India and from Labour Party members of the cabinet to grant political concessions. The American Government also supported the pressure for political concessions.[179] In March 1942 Labour member of the war cabinet, Sir Staffort Cripps, succeeded in getting the cabinet to make a draft declaration which promised India Dominion Status with the right of secession after the war. Furthermore, it suggested a constitution-making body to be elected by the provincial legislatures and individual provinces would be given the right not to join.[180] In Punjab the draft declaration was received with concern. The newly appointed Governor of the Punjab, Sir Bertrand Glancy expressed his worries that questions regarding India's future constitution might create fear among the Muslims of being dominated by the Hindus and therefore endanger their ability to work effectively for the defence of British India. "Recruitment will be very seriously affected as all communities will wish to keep their young men at home to defend their own interest".[181] The Viceroy was afraid that Sikh fear of Muslim dominance in a separate Punjab might result in Sikhs getting "troublesome", which again would make Muslims "look to their own defence".[182] It was therefore agreed to postpone

---

179. Anita Inder Singh, op., cit., p. 73.
180. Sumit Sarkar, op., cit., p. 386
181. Glancy to Linlithgow, Transfer of Power (henceforth TOP) vol. 1, p. 321.
182. Linlithgow to Amery, TOP vol. 1., pp. 340-341 .

making the draft declaration on official British policy and instead send a mission to India to explore reactions to the draft.[183] On 23rd March Cripps left for India to start negotiations with the Indian leaders. Viceroy Lintithgow, who was strongly against the draft declaration, threatened to resign, but was pacified by Prime Minister Winston Churchill, who made it clear that, in his view, the mission was only embarked upon to underline the sincerity of the British Government.[184]

On 9th April Cripps seemed very close in reaching a political agreement. A compromise on who should be in control of the Indian defence had been worked out. The defence department was proposed to be led by an Indian and the field operations by a British Commander-in-Chief. However, while the Congress was in favour of such an agreement it was strongly ruled out by Churchill and Linlithgow. The negotiations subsequently broke down and Cripps returned to England. Even though his mission had failed, the draft declaration emphasised that India's independence was within the reach and that individual provinces, like Punjab, could decide not to be part of an Indian Federation. The major question however, was whether a separate Pakistan would emerge eventually.

---

183. Ayesha Jalal, op., cit., p. 73.
184. Sumit Sarkar, op., cit., 386.

Summary

The introduction of provincial self-government and the extension of franchise in 1937 were followed by an outbreak of communal violence in Punjab between 1937-1939. While intra-community clashes also took place, most of the incidents were related to the inter-communal violence. These clashes generally rallied around religious customs and offences like cow slaughtering, prayer calls and procession routes. The intra-communal violence was connected with political disagreement as between Hindu nationalists and Hindu Congress members or between pro-Congress and anti-Congress Muslims. Another difference lay in the degree of violence. The intra-community violence was less both in frequency and scope, while the inter-community violence had a higher frequency and many casualties. Thus, the increasing political participation and the emerging political power struggle spilled over to the religious field and triggered off communalism and communal violence. In this connection it is important to remember that communalism did not necessarily embrace all of society, but only "touched limited groups in certain areas".[185] Besides, communities could shift from being engaged in a religious feud at one moment to living in harmony the next, which shows that it was still cases of 'traditional violence' that occurred.

---

185. Mushirul Hasan: "Introduction" in Mushirul Hasan (1993) op., cit., p. 34.

However, there was developing a continuing tension among Hindus, Sikhs and Muslims with disagreements not only regarding procession routes but also concerning representation in the municipal services. Jinnah's Lahore resolution on 22nd March 1940 and the political call for a separate Muslim state, Pakistan, generated fear and mistrust among Sikhs and Hindus and paved the way for a strengthening of the volunteer corps. The possibility of exercising violence was now beginning to be institutionalised. The hardening of the conflict was also expressed by the mutual accusations of attempts to obtain a Hindu Raj or Muslim Raj. An increasingly limited space was left for co-operation among the communities at the political level and for a democratic discourse and interaction as the general tone became more and more irreconcilable. By the end of 1941, Sikh leaders were calling for 'resisting Pakistan by force'.

In 1940-1942 many people did not understand what Pakistan was about but Sikhs and Hindus perceived it as a threat against them (the same way as Muslims were afraid of Hindu domination). It changed the character of the communal strife firstly, by further polarising the communities and secondly, by making territory and religion the basic political issues. The concept of the multicultural Punjab disappeared with the concept of an Islamic Pakistan.

The British were very much aware of the hardening of the conflict but their major concern was that it should not affect the war effort. The British preoccupation with the war, while trying to keep the demands for Indian independence in the background, coupled with a limited interest in the deteriorating communal relations, allowed the communal violence to take deeper roots in an already divided society.

Chapter 2
Interim

From the Cripps Mission to the 1946 Provincial Election

Though no violent incident was reported in the first half of April 1942, a clear worsening of communal relations was detected in the aftermath of the failure of the Cripps Mission in reaching an agreement. The Hindu volunteer organisation, RSS, had a remarkable increase in membership and a considerable expansion in its activities. The Akali Sikhs had created a corp's d'elite with special uniforms and reorganised the Sikh community on a quasi-military footing. The Congressmen persisted in proclaiming that the people should not look to Government agencies for protection in times of emergency, but instead band themselves into volunteer brigades under the Congress's direction.[186]

Whether these groups were only defensive in nature was uncertain, as it was difficult to ascertain whether leaders of volunteer bodies "could or would restrain their followers in times of serious communal unrest".[187] In this atmosphere

---

186. FR first half of April 1942, IOL L/P&J/5/245, p. 95.
187. FR second half of April 1942, IOL L/P&J/5/245, p. 88.

of suspicion and tension the communal defence organisations were growing like "mushrooms".[188] In June it was reported that fears of communal unrest caused more anxiety than the threat of an Axis invasion.[189] This picture changed slightly the following month. The German successes in neighbouring Caucasus together with worries of a Japanese attack generated feelings of uneasiness and fear.[190] Thus, the communal unrest was held at bay from July to September even though the cleavage among the three communities was reportedly expanding.

However, at the political centre stage the battle between the British and the Congress reached a new high. On 8th August the All India Congress Committee passed a resolution for civil disobedience called 'Quit India'.[191] The British response to the resolution was swift and in the following days all central leaders, including Nehru and Gandhi were arrested. By this use of force the British managed to suppress the movement and by the end of 1942 it was at the edge of having petered out.[192] In Punjab the 'Quit India' campaign contributed to the description of 1942 as a year full of communal tension, though devoid of any major incidents. On the contrary the year ended peacefully

188. FR second half of May 1942, IOL L/P&J/5/245, p. 75.
189. FR second half of June 1942, IOL L/P&J/5/245, p. 64.
190. FR second half of July 1942, IOL L/P&J/5/245, p. 50.
191. B. R. Nanda: "Nehru, the Indian National Congress and the Partition of India, 1935-47", in C. H. Philips & M. D. Wainwright (eds.): The Partition of India, Policies and perspectives, 1935-47, London 1971, p. 171.
192. Sumit Sarkar, op., cit., p. 388.

and it was reported that the "improvements in news from the war effort" everywhere had resulted in "greater confidence in allied victory".[193]

However, the death of Premier, Sir Sikander Hyat Khan in December 1942 was a big blow to the British.[194] Sir Sikander, who was followed by Khizar Tiwana Khan, had been a very important British ally. And even though Jinnah did not have any say in his replacement, it was certain that Sir Sikander's death would make it easier for Jinnah to challenge the Unionist leadership in Punjab. The new leadership was also challenged within the Unionist Party by a group of young rural based Muslim leaders, who were opposed to Khizar and had started moving towards the viewpoints of the Muslim League.[195]

Disregarding the change in political leadership, the year 1943 began on a peaceful note. No communal incidents were reported and the public morale remained high since everybody was expecting an Allied victory.[196] It was only in April that a communal clash was reported from Ambala district, where a group of Muslims had attacked a group of *Nihangs* or the Sikh warriors, leaving seven people

193. FR second half of December 1942, IOL L/P&J/5/245, p 2.
194. Anita Inder Singh, op., cit., p. 94.
195. David Gilmartin: "Religious Leadership and the Pakistan Movement in the Punjab", MAS, 13, 3 (1979), pp. 506-507.
196. FR second half of January 1943 & FR first half of March 1943, IOL, L/P&J/5/246, p. 122 & p. 106.

injured.[197] However, the weakening of the Unionists after Sikander's death was already evident in May.[198] The economic situation in the Punjab, especially the fall in agricultural prices, was now the main pre-occupation of its people.[199] For the Unionist Government the heavy army recruitment and the rationing of food-grains resulted in a decrease in popularity in the countryside.[200] In January 1944, at Haripur in the neighbouring North West Frontier Province (NWFP), a major riot between Sikhs and Muslims threatened the communal situation in Punjab as well. The Congress apparently used the incident to emphasise the impossibility of Sikh/Muslim co-operation and was accused by the Akalis of having instigated the riot themselves.[201] While the month of February was eventless, two incidents were mentioned in the beginning of March. The first one took place in the Hissar district where eight Muslims were killed and one wounded in a Hindu - Muslim clash. The second one was in Lahore city where a Hindu stabbed one Muslim to death.[202]

The communal relations and the Unionist leadership in the Punjab were also threatened by Jinnah's aggressive

---

197. FR first half of April 1943, IOL, L/P&J/5/246, p. 93.
198. Ayesha Jalal, op., cit., p. 86.
199. FR second half of August 1943, IOL, L/P&J/5/246, p. 48 & FR first half of October 1943, IOL, L/P&J/5/246, p. 27.
200. Ian Talbot: Provincial Politics and the Pakistan Movement (1988), op., cit., p. 93.
201. FR first half of January 1944, IOL, L/P&J/5/247, p. 125.
202. FR first half of March 1944, IOL, L/P&J/5/247, p. 108.

posture. During a meeting at the end of March with members of the Muslim League, Jinnah denied the existence of the Sikander-Jinnah pact and stated that such a thing as a Unionist Party did not exist. Even though Jinnah had failed to convince everybody present, the Viceroy feared "that in the long run the economic alignment may be substituted for the communal alignment in Punjab politics".[203] Moreover, an attempt by Jinnah to establish a Muslim League coalition ministry in Punjab was regarded as a threat to the communal peace.[204] The battle between Jinnah and Khizar broke out fully in April when negotiations between them broke down. Subsequently they started thundering at each other through the columns of the press.[205] In May 1944 the final break between the Unionists and Jinnah took place when Khizar was expelled from the Muslim League.[206] By calling off the Sikander-Jinnah pact of 1937 and expelling Khizar Khan from the league, Jinnah showed that he was getting ready to enter Punjabi politics. Having, more or less, consolidated his position as representative of Muslims at the centre, it was now time to turn to the Muslim majority provinces. Furthermore, Jinnah had no longer a political interest in upholding an agreement from 1937 that had partly been made to keep him out of Punjabi politics.

According to David Gilmartin, one reason for Jinnah's

---

203. Wavell to Amery, TOP vol. 4, pp. 844-850.
204. FR second half of April 1944, IOL, L/P&J/5/247, p. 88.
205. Ian Talbot: Khizar Tiwana. (1996), op., cit., p. 111.
206. Ayesha Jalal, op., cit., p. 95.

growing success in the Punjab was that those Muslim leaders who entered politics during the 1940s did not want to submit to the Unionist Party: "After Sir Sikander's death, they had turned to the Pakistan idea as a new focus for their politics, and a new cultural foundation for their claim to provincial influence".[207] One of the first to shift his allegiance from the Unionist to the Muslim League was Mian Mumtaz Daulatana, who joined the League in 1943. He was later followed by Shaukat Hyat Khan (son of the late Sikander Hyat Khan) who joined the Muslim League, after he was dismissed from the Unionist ministry in 1944. What Jinnah provided these and others with was a way to upset the political balance. He wanted to bring down the Government and form a purely Muslim League Ministry. This attempt caused concern among the British who felt that outside involvement in the Punjab affair would make the matters worse. However, it is significant that even though Jinnah's task was political, it was conducted through the use of religious propaganda. The politicians were clearly appropriating the symbols used in the traditional religious conflict. It also demonstrated, as argued by Ian Talbot, "the existence of a 'Muslim' community with its separate political interest".[208] However, one should remember that even after Khizar was expelled from the League in May 1994 a majority of Muslim Unionists stayed with him.[209]

---

207. David Gilmartin (1988), op., cit., p. 192.
208. Ian Talbot: Freedom's Cry. (1996), op. cit., p. 70.
209. Anita Inder Singh, op., cit., p. 105.

While the intra-communal battle for political power between the Muslim League and the Unionists intensified, the inter-communal clashes continued too. At the end of May, a group of Muslims had stabbed a Hindu bookbinder to death and his house was burned down. In another incident, Muslims attacked two Sikh spectators at a religious fair in Multan district because they were sitting in such a manner that their feet were placed above the ceiling of a Muslim shrine. In the subsequent clash two Sikhs died and five were injured.[210]

Though the joy of the Allied landing in Normandy and the progress of the Soviet Army was emphasised in the fortnightly report, the main concern in the summer of 1944 continued to be the deteriorating communal and political relations among the three communities and the main political parties. Viceroy Wavell wrote that even though the Punjab appeared calm, Governor Glancy was worried about the possible activities of the Muslim League National Guards, a body formed by a reorganisation of the Muslim League volunteers. At an All India Muslim League meeting in May 1944 the constitution for the volunteer organisation was altered. It was now emphasised that the raison d'être of the organisation was to strengthen the social and physical development of Muslims and create a spirit of self-sacrifice and service. Another change was that members of the newly

---

210. FR second half of May 1944, IOL, L/P&J/5/247, p. 77.

formed Muslim League National Guard would be wearing uniform.[211] Thus, the quasi-military character of the organisation was underlined.

According to the Governor it was important to make it clear from the very beginning that uniformed bodies of this kind would not be tolerated. The Viceroy stated that "the law as it stands prohibits drilling and other training of a military kind, and we may have to tighten it up".[212] In a conversation with the Viceroy in June, Khizar expressed his apprehensions about the Muslim League National Guards and Jinnah's use of religious propaganda.[213] However, nothing was done against the volunteer organisations.

That members of the volunteer organisations were participating in communal fights was evident on 4th July, when 15 young Hindus, two of whom were connected to the RSS, attacked four Muslim butchers causing two of them minor injuries.[214] On 24th July a Hindu woman's conversion to Islam triggered off a very serious clash at Farrukhnagar in Gurgaon district in Southwest Punjab. Reportedly more than two thousand Hindus from neighbouring villages gathered and killed 8 Muslims, injured 16 others and did considerable damage to Muslims houses.[215] The incident

211. Ian Talbot: Freedom's Cry. (1996), op., cit., p. 64.
212. Wavell to Amery, TOP vol. 4, pp. 1019-1023.
213. Wavell to Amery, TOP vol. 4, pp. 1033-1036.
214. FR first half of July 1944, IOL, L/P&J/5/247, p. 61.
215. FR second half of July 1944, IOL, L/P&J/5/247, p. 57.

testified not only to the growing communal tension but also that women were regarded more as community property than as private individuals.

In the second half of September 1944, two minor communal incidents were reported. In the first incident that occurred on the 15th, Hindus playing music close to a mosque were attacked by stone throwing Muslims, and on the 24th, a Dussehra procession[216] (Hindu procession) was attacked by Muslims because it came too close to a mosque which was calling the Azzan.[217] Even though 1944 ended without any major clashes it was evident that the space for peaceful coexistence was getting smaller. In the fortnightly reports it was assumed that the violence would increase.[218] Nevertheless 1945 began without any reports of communal incidents.[219] In the end of April, however, a minor incident occurred in the city of Amritsar when two Muslims were attacked by RSS volunteers leaving one of the Muslims wounded from stabbing.[220] Still peace was maintained in Punjab and no communal incidents were reported either from May, June, July or August,[221] i.e. during the final months of the war.

---

216. The festival of Dusshera is celebrated at the end of a 9 day long worship which culminates into a battle between good and evil on the tenth day. The procession marks the victory of good.
217. FR second half of September 1944, IOL, L/P&J/5/247, p. 36.
218. FR first half of November 1944, IOL, L/P&J/5/247, p. 21.
219. FR second half of January 1945 & FR first half of March 1945, IOL L/P&J/5/248, p. 113 & p. 97.
220. FR second half of April 1945, IOL L/P&J/5/248, p. 79.
221. See FR from first and second half of May, June, July and August, IOL, L/P&J/5/248, p. 45-66.

On 15th June Viceroy Wavell announced that talks on forming a new executive council were going to be held and even though the Congress was opposed to the idea of parity between Caste Hindus and Muslims in the proposed council, they decided to attend. On 25th June the conference opened in Simla.[222] But before it could start debating the political future of India it was faced with the problem of selecting the Council members. Jinnah who was afraid of Muslims being outvoted by a combination of Caste Hindus, Scheduled Caste Hindus and Sikhs, proposed a Muslim veto. But he didn't stop there. He demanded that the Muslim League should have the right to nominate all Muslim members to the Council. For the Punjab Premier, Khizar Tiwana Khan, a Congress - League parity was looked upon with concern because, if the League got the right to nominate all Muslims, it would totally sideline the Unionists.[223] In view of these incompatible interests Viceroy Wavell decided, on 14th July, to close the conference.

The political leadership in England changed soon after and in the July election the Labour Party came to power, which was perceived in India as a political advantage.[224] The failure of the Simla Conference persuaded the Labour Cabinet that an interim settlement wouldn't work. Instead they started arguing for a final settlement, where no minority

---

222. Anita Inder Singh, op., cit., p. 119.
223. Ayesha Jalal, op., cit., p. 128.
224. FR second half of July 1945, IOL, L/P&J/5/248, p. 53.

would have a veto but where the Muslim majority provinces would not be forced into a settlement that they were against.[225] For Jinnah it meant the need to strengthen his Muslim League before the coming provincial elections. And on 21st August 1945 Viceroy Wavell announced that provincial elections were soon going to take place.

In the Punjab the call for election was looked upon with great concern due to the Muslim League's propaganda. Jinnah was being hailed as the champion of Islam and Governor Glancy expressed his worry that the forthcoming provincial elections would be held on an entirely false issue. "The uninformed Muslim will be told that the question he is called on to answer at the polls is - Are you a true believer or an infidel and a traitor?"[226] According to Glancy, the Unionist wouldn't have any countermove against this claim and he feared that the consequences of the election could be devastating. "I have discussed the general situation with a variety of people, officials and non-officials, European and Indian: the consensus of opinion is that, if Pakistan becomes an imminent reality, we shall be heading straight for a bloodshed on a wide scale."[227] It is worth noting that the British officialdom was fully aware of the potential of massive violence should Pakistan be established.

225. Ayesha Jalal, op.cit., p. 132.
226. Glancy to Wavell, Simla 16th August 1945, TOP vol. 6, pp. 71-72.
227. Ibid.

For the time being, however, the Punjab remained peaceful and in the first half of September only two minor communal incidents were reported. The first incident occurred in the city of Lahore on 30th August, where a Muslim was manhandled and stabbed in retaliation for making fun of Hindu women going to a temple. In the second incident, on 7th September, 14 people were injured during a Hindu - Muslim clash which was triggered off due to the disagreement over the construction of a wall.[228]

However, as the election propaganda, which was focused on the possibility of a Pakistan, started accelerating "the possibility of serious and widespread riots",[229] also increased. According to Glancy the communal relations were deteriorating because of fear of secession of the Punjab and he wanted Wavell to give a statement clarifying that what Cripps in 1942 had defined as a province, was not necessarily how a province was to be defined now. Such statement would counter the "erroneous" doctrine of "Islam in danger", and prevent the elections to be held on a false pretext, besides, "avert the chances of civil war to which, as it seems to me [Glancy], we are daily drifting nearer as things stand as present".[230] But in a letter to a member of the British Cabinet, two days later, Wavell rejected the idea of giving such a statement. Wavell also enclosed a letter

---

228. FR first half of September 1945, IOL, L/P&J/5/248, p. 39.
229. FR first half of October 1945, IOL, L/P&J/5/248, p. 25.
230. Glancy to Wavell, Lahore 27th October 1945, TOP vol. 6, pp. 413-414.

dated 23rd October from Master Tara Singh, a Sikh leader, to the British Prime Minister Clement Attlee.

Tara Singh wanted Attlee to appreciate the worsening communal situation and wrote that it would be unfair if the small Muslim majority should decide the future of all the Punjabis. He further mentioned that only three out of the five divisions in Punjab had a Muslim majority. "Non-Muslims, especially the Sikhs, are quite determined to resist - if necessary, by force of arms - being included in Pakistan, or being put under any sort of communal domination".[231] The Sikh opposition to the creation of a Pakistan further increased during the second half of 1945. While Muslims were united for an Islamic homeland, the Sikhs and Hindus were united against it. For the Sikhs, especially, it was important that the Punjab remained as multi-religious as possible. Even though their rhetoric was directed against a Pakistan and the creation of a Muslim state, their main fear was to be politically subjugated either by a Muslim or a Hindu majority after independence.[232]

The hardening of the political rhetoric during the election campaign resulted in fear of a breakdown of the fragile communal peace.[233] By the end of November a riot

231. Wavell to Pethick-Lawrence, New Delhi 29th October 1945, TOP vol. 6, pp. 420-424.
232. Tan Tai Young: "Prelude to Partition: Sikh Responses to the Demand for Pakistan", International Journal of Punjab Studies, 1, 2 (1994), pp. 190-191.
233. FR second half of October 1945, IOL, L/P&J/5/248, p. 22.

was reported from the Gurgaon district in south-eastern Punjab, where a group of Muslims allegedly brought a cart full of beef meat through a Hindu bazaar. In the subsequent clash 27 Hindus and 23 Muslims were injured.[234] In the last report from the year it was stated that the situation had gradually deteriorated owing to the communal propaganda of political parties for electioneering purposes.[235]

The pre-election tension continued throughout the beginning of 1946.[236] In the following Fatwa[237] from Nawa-e-waqt, the leader of the Hazrat Shah Nur Jamal shrine it was announced that: "I command all those people who are in my *silsilah,* or the following, to do everything possible to help the Muslim League and give their votes to it. All those people who do not act accordingly to this message should consider themselves no longer members of my *silsilah*".[238] And in the beginning of February, it was reported that Muslims were threatened with excommunication if they did not vote for the Muslim League, along with an "increase of fanaticism evinced by the speeches of Muslim League leaders".[239] The tenants and labourers were also put under pressure from their landlords to vote for the League and

---

234. FR second half of November 1945, IOL, L/P&J/5/248, p. 13.
235. FR second half of December 1945, IOL, L/P&J/5/248, p. 2.
236. FR first half of January 1946, IOL, L/P&J/5/249, p. 160.
237. Fatwa is an edict issued by the Imam, the religious head of the order.
238. Quoted in Ian Talbot: Provincial Politics and the Pakistan Movement. (1988), op., cit., p. 99.
239. Governor's report dated 2nd February 1946, IOL, L/P&J/5/249, p. 153.

clan networks were used to mobilise the rural voters.[240] Even though no violent outbreaks took place up to the announcement of the election result in the end of February, it was reported that the Muslim League election propaganda had strained the communal relations.[241]

Summary

The period in Punjab from the departure of Cripps Mission in April 1942 to the provincial elections in 1945/46 could be aptly characterised as an interim period. The division among the three communities was expressed through the increase in membership of the volunteer groups. As even the Congress was urging people to organise volunteer groups the people obviously doubted the Government's ability to protect them. The great German and Japanese victories in 1942 created the fear of an invasion of British India and exposed the vulnerability of the Colonial state. However, the communal unrest in the Punjab was held at bay. At the All India level the Congress opposition to British rule was intensified by the massive 'Quit India' movement, which eventually was effectively put down by the use of force.

In terms of violent clashes from 1942 until the end of the war, the Punjab remained relatively calm. The only major incident was a widespread riot in connection with a Hindu

---

240. Ian Talbot: Punjab and the Raj.(1988), op., cit., p. 208.
241. FR second half of February 1946, IOL, L/P&J/5/249, p. 142.

woman's conversion to Islam. However, in the fortnightly reports and other sources the officials continuously expressed concern about the growing tension among the three communities. Especially the increase in mobilisation and the stronger organisation of people into the quasi-military volunteer groups was widely reflected upon in the fortnightly reports. While the RSS and the Sikh bodies had operated in the Punjab before the war, the Muslim League volunteer group in 1944 was reorganised as the Muslim League National Guards. This showed how the League was attempting to monopolise the Muslim community. That the Muslim League was getting more powerful was evident in the inability of the Punjab Government to prohibit the Muslim League National Guards, even though the law made it possible to disallow such an organisation. At the political level in Punjab the Muslim League was also making headway, as the unionist leadership was heavily challenged by a growing support for the League amongst regional Muslim leaders. The untimely dead of Sir Sikander Hyat Khan in December 1942 and the inability of his successor, Khizar Tiwana Khan, in sustaining Jinnah's pressure, further paved the way for increased influence for the league in the Punjab.

The provincial election campaign in 1945 was rallied around religious issues like "Islam in danger" but the central theme was the possibility of creating a separate Pakistan. The politicisation of religion was most clearly emphasised by the threat of excommunication of Muslims who did not vote for the Muslim League. The threat sealed the union between politics and religion while effectively completing the communalisation process.

Chapter 3
New Escalation

From the 1946
Elections till Early 1947

The result of the provincial elections in Punjab, which was announced in February 1946, showed a major victory for the Muslim League. They polled 75 seats and emerged as the single largest party in the assembly.[242] The second winner was the Congress Party with 51 seats, while the Unionists came in third with 21 seats. As compared to the 1937 election, where the Unionist Party had won an absolute majority, this election showed that All India parties now dominated Punjabi politics and that the Unionists had been sidelined by the electorates. However, with 75 seats in the assembly the Muslim League was still 13 seats short of the majority figure of 88. So even though badly decimated, the Unionist Party could remain in office and Khizar Tiwana Khan continued as Premier. On 7th March he formed a new Government with the support of the Akalis and the Congress.[243] Thus, notwithstanding its huge victory the Muslim League found itself in opposition and therefore

---

242. For the election result in Punjab see Ayesha Jalal, op., cit., p. 150.
243. Anita Inder Singh, op., cit., p. 141.

continued the uncompromising rhetoric of the election campaign. In March 1946 it was reported that. "The propaganda of the Muslim League was tantamount to incitement of violence".[244]

On 18th March at Jandiala in Amritsar district, one Muslim was killed and eight injured in a Muslim-Sikh clash.[245] In April the situation had deteriorated even further and reportedly, all parties were equipping themselves with crude weapons. The membership of the RSS had risen sharply because of the physical training classes and exercises, which were being regularly held in most of the main cities in the province.[246] The same fortnightly report also stated that it looked as if the Muslim League and the RSS were getting ready to go to war with each other.[247] Such war like preparations increased in the beginning of May. In the Punjab and other Muslim majority provinces, the Muslim League National Guards was reinforced and ex-military servicemen called upon to enlist in the force.[248] The membership of the RSS was growing, as was the number of drills and assemblies, particularly in Muslim areas.[249] It further fuelled the growth of the private armies and they became bolder in their defiance of law.[250] It was concluded

244. Governor's report dated 15th March 1946, IOL, L/P&J/5/249, p. 139.
245. FR second half of March 1946, IOL, L/P&J/5/249, p. 131.
246. FR second half of April 1946, IOL, L/P&J/5/249, p. 117.
247. Ibid.
248. Anita Inder Singh, op., cit., p. 153.
249. FR first half of May 1946, IOL, L/P&J/5/249, p. 111.
250. FR second half of May 1946, IOL, L/P&J/5/249, p. 104.

that only the imposition of curfew could keep the Muslims and Hindus away from each other, more so in view of the reports of deliberate attacks on womenfolk in the Punjab.[251] Interestingly, the fortnightly report did not elaborate on the nature of the attacks. The emphasis was not on what had happened to the women but on how these attacks affected the communities.

The targeting of women in communal conflicts is extremely significant, as it emphasises a beginning of shift in the nature of violence. Women were introduced as new actors (mostly passive) in such conflicts. This differentiated the present conflict from the traditional riots, which were essentially conducted in a male domain i.e., between men of opposing religious identities and in the public space. Veena Das suggests, "each riot leaves its signature, and one way to decipher this is to pay attention to the spaces involved".[252] The spaces may be broadly defined as issues, location or the actors involved. From 1946 onwards, the riots were no longer viewed 'business as usual' mainly because issues changed from protection of religious places and symbols to that of state formation; the location of violence was not just limited to urban areas, but engulfed the rural areas as well and lastly; the actors involved were not just men, but also women and children, though mostly as victims.

---

251. Ibid.
252. Veena Das, "Introduction" in Veena Das (ed)., Mirrors of Violence: Communities, Riots and Survivors in South Asia, Delhi, 1990, p. 11.

However, the month of June witnessed an improvement in the communal relations as the level of tension among the communities lowered. In the fortnightly report this development was explained as an awareness of the consequences if major communal riots occurred.[253] Nevertheless, the growth of the private communal armies continued unabated. The new Governor of Punjab Sir Evan Jenkins forwarded in a telegram the Sikh anxiety about their future position in the Punjab. If they could not be granted safeguards they would turn to agitation, which was likely to be of a violent nature.[254]

At the beginning of July an increase in the activities of both the RSS and the Muslim League National Guards was reported. Whereas the membership of the RSS was believed to have doubled since November last year and was now estimated at 28.000, the membership of the Muslim League National Guards had increased from three thousand at the end of 1945 to more than ten thousand, i.e. more than tripled in six months.[255] The fortnightly reports also mentioned that both the RSS and the Muslim League National Guards were spreading rumours which posed a potential danger, especially now when they were represented in almost every district in the Punjab. The RSS particularly, was referred to as getting more involved in the violence

---

253. FR first half of June 1946, IOL, L/P&J/5/249, p. 96.
254. Jenkins to Wavell, Telegram sent 26th June 1946, TOP vol. 7, pp. 1065-1066.
255. FR first half of July 1946, IOL, L/P&J/5/249, p. 85.

and it was assumed that Punjab would blow up, unless the political situation improved.[256]

Against the backdrop of the political and communal turmoil after the provincial elections, the British decided to make a new attempt to initiate negotiations about a new Indian constitution. On 14th March the Cabinet Mission, which consisted of Sir Staffort Cripps, Secretary of State for India Pethick-Lawrence and A. V. Alexander arrived in India. After the initial talks, it was evident to the Mission that an agreement on an interim Government was impossible prior to an agreement on the political structure of an independent India. The Mission proposed a structure with a weak centre controlling only defence, communication and foreign affairs, while the existing provincial assemblies should be grouped into three sections. There should be one section for the Hindu majority provinces, one for the Muslim majority provinces of the northwest and one for the Muslim majority provinces of the northeast. Each of the three sections was to continue having a legislature of their own.[257] On 6th June the Muslim League accepted the plan and on 24th the Congress followed suit. However, both acceptances were given in accordance to their own interpretations.

The major area of disagreement was whether the grouping of provinces in the two Muslim sections should

---

256. FR first half of August 1946, IOL, L/P&J/5/249, p. 71.
257. Sumit Sarkar, op., cit., p. 430.

be compulsory or not. For the Muslim League, compulsory grouping was essential since it would consolidate their power in the Muslim majority areas. The Congress, however, was strongly opposed to compulsory grouping because it would make it impossible for provinces to leave the section. On 10th July Congress President Nehru declared that the only commitment his Party had given "was to participate in the Constituent Assembly elections".[258] The response from Jinnah to Nehru's statement came on 30th July when the Muslim League withdrew their earlier acceptance of the Cabinet Mission plan. Instead they called for a 'Direct Action' from 16th August "to achieve Pakistan".[259]

The mass Muslim movement of "Direct Action" triggered off the worst rioting in India after the war. The north-eastern province, Bengal, was particularly affected and the main city, Calcutta, turned into an inferno. Muslims and Hindus clashed in the streets between 16th and 20th of August. The rioting was started by a section of Muslims propagating the creation of Pakistan by "direct and forceful action".[260] But during the course of the rioting, all communities were equally involved. When the violence subsided the numbers of victims had to be counted in thousands. According to the official estimates 4,000 were

258. Ibid.
259. Ibid. For a more elaborate account of the Cabinet Mission negotiations, see; Ayesha Jalal, op., cit., pp. 174-207. & Anita Inder Singh, op., cit., pp. 142-178.
260. Suranjan Das, op., cit., p. 169

dead and 10,000 injured.[261] In October 1946 massive rioting broke out in Noakhali and Tippera, two south-eastern districts in Bengal. Prior to this event neither district had experienced any major Hindu-Muslim "outburst".[262] However, the spiral of communal violence did not limit itself to the Bengal. Bombay in the southwest of India experienced rioting in early September and so did the province of Bihar and United Province in the northern and central part in of India in late October and in November. Especially the Bihar riots were brutal. In retaliation to the Hindus killed in Noakhali, Hindu peasants massacred more than 7,000 Muslims. Nehru was horrified and remarked. "A madness has seized the people".[263]

So far the Punjab had managed to stay clear of the mass violence. The massive loss of lives in Calcutta from 16th till 20th August did not have any immediate impact on the belligerent feelings among the three communities in the Punjab. In the fortnightly report it was stated, "civil war is still accepted as being preferable to the abandoning of any principle and the Calcutta casualties are regarded as little or nothing compared with what is likely to happen if a political agreement is not reached".[264]

Along with the Cabinet Mission negotiations Viceroy

---

261. Ibid., p. 171.
262. Ibid., p. 193.
263. Sumit Sarkar, op., cit., p. 433.
264. FR second half of August 1946, IOL, L/P&J/5/249, p. 57.

Wavell conducted his own talks with the Indian leaders about setting up an interim Government at the centre. This was met with obstacles from Jinnah who demanded parity between the Congress and the League and the right to nominate all Muslims as during the failed Simla negotiations in June/July 1945. Reiterating his fear of Muslim representatives being marginalized by Hindus and Sikhs, he felt very displeased with the proposal for the interim Government. Of the total of 14 members, six would be nominated by the Congress, five by the Muslim League and three by the minorities, including one Sikh. Thus, Jinnah was neither granted parity with the Congress nor the right to nominate all Muslims.[265] The only concession to him was that no regional Muslims leaders were included. Jinnah refused to accept anything less than parity with the Congress and at an All India Muslim League meeting in Bombay on 28th July it was decided not to participate in the interim Government at all.

Thus, on 6th August, Nehru was called by the Viceroy to form the Government,[266] and on 2nd September 1946 a Congress dominated interim Government was sworn in and was "greeted with the threat of direct action by the League".[267] At the centre the hostility between the Muslim League and the Congress increased subsequently and there

---

265. Ayesha Jalal, op., cit., p. 210.
266. Ibid., p. 214.
267. Anita Inder Singh, op., cit., p. 190.

were no signs of will to negotiate or compromise on either side. In Punjab the Muslim League called on all "able-bodied Muslims to enlist in the National Guard".[268] However, due to Muslim restrain, the inauguration of the interim Government was not followed by any disturbances in the Punjab.[269]

Nevertheless, Muslims were frightened and felt betrayed by the British for handing over the power to the Congress. Furthermore, Muslims felt antagonised by the Hindu propaganda about the Calcutta killings. They felt that only Muslims were blamed and did not "relish cartoons of Muslim League leaders washing in blood, cutting off the breast of Hindu women, and committing other atrocities".[270] On the other hand, the Hindus were jubilant. They believed that now with British help, they would be able to suppress the Muslims in Punjab once and for all. Governor Jenkins described the Hindu newspapers as both arrogant and communal in their tone. The Sikh position was, however, more uncertain. While some were in alliance with the Congress, others felt reluctant to finally break with the Muslims. But in case of disturbances, Sikhs were expected to side with the Hindus.[271]

Regarding the general political situation at the

268. Ibid.
269. FR first half of September 1946, IOL, L/P&J/5/249, p. 49.
270. Jenkins to Wavell, 31st August 1946, TOP vol. 8, pp. 158-164.
271. Ibid.

provincial level, the Governor's analysis was, that the Khizar Ministry had lost all respect: "It has failed to control the bitterly communal press, turned a blind eye on 'private armies' [and] permitted speeches advocating revolution and murder".[272] In Jenkins opinion the only way to handle the communal situation competently, was if the Khizar Ministry started to deal firmly not only with the Muslim supporters of the League but also with its own followers. The Government would have to confront the communal press, take action against violent speakers disregarding their party affiliations and suppress private armies, especially the Muslim League National Guards and the RSS. It was also expected to deal firmly with lawlessness of all kind and make clear by action and not by statements their willingness to use law and order powers when needed.[273]

However, the Government took no initiative and the communal tension continued unabated. In the end of September a communal incident was reported at Hansi in the Hissar district in connection with a *Dussehra* procession. One person was killed and 25 injured. However, it was also reported that there had been an improvement in the communal relations in several other places and that this probably was due to a combination of police control and deterrence. While the first half of October went by peacefully,

---

272. Ibid.
273. Ibid.

communal clashes were reported from the city of Ludhiana between 25th and 27th October which left nine people dead and 25 injured.[274] In the town of Rohtak a clash between Hindus and Muslims was reported at the beginning of November with 16 people killed and 18 injured. The rumours about communal disorder resulted in the formation of new communal bodies and further strengthening of the Muslim League National Guards and the RSS. These bodies were not only getting more popular but also more active and belligerent.[275] The Sikhs, however, were trying to act neutral.

On 17th November a clash between Hindus and Muslims left 23 people killed.[276] Governor Jenkins again expressed his concern over the communal situation, which he described as "very bad indeed" and restated his desire to ban the private armies.[277] However, the month of December reported some improvement in the communal situation,[278] and it was stated that the communal relations were now better than they had been for months.[279] Nevertheless, it was emphasised that tension could easily rise and that the communal damage done during 1946 was unlikely to be repaired.[280]

---

274. FR second half of October 1946, IOL, L/P&J/5/249, p. 31.
275. FR first half of November 1946, IOL, L/P&J/5/249, p. 25.
276. FR second half of November 1946, IOL, L/P&J/5/249, p. 20.
277. Jenkins to Colville, 30th November 1946, TOP vol. 9, pp. 229-230.
278. FR first half of December 1946, IOL, L/P&J/5/249, p. 21.
279. FR second half of December 1946, IOL, L/P&J/5/249, p. 9.
280. Ibid.

In January 1947 a similar picture prevailed. The situation "is unfortunately devoid of genuine improvements and continues to be serious with communal ill feeling as deep-seated and bitter as ever".[281] Another major problem was communal disturbances in the neighbouring provinces. The inflow of refugees and the many rumours that followed escalated the tension and though officials were trying to guard the border zealously, it was impossible to exclude stories of violence.[282]

As a measure to control the explosive situation the Punjab Government declared the Muslim League National Guards and the RSS illegal on 24th January. However, this decision by the Khizar Ministry created turbulent scenes and unrest in the province. The Government's decision was motivated by the unsatisfactory state of communal feelings, and it declared private armies a danger to the peace.[283] Governor Jenkins strongly supported the ban. He argued that both the RSS and the Muslim League National Guards were communal bodies and were organised on communal lines. The RSS members were recruited from among orthodox Hindus while members of the Muslim league National Guards were recruited from the Muslim League.[284]

After the imposition of the ban, seven Muslim League

281. FR first half of January 1947, IOL, L/P&J/5/250, p. 98.
282. Ibid.
283. FR second half of January 1947, IOL, L/P&J/5/250, p. 90.
284. Jenkins to Pethick-Lawrence, 26th January 1947, TOP vol. 9, pp. 556-557.

leaders were arrested since they did not follow the Government ban. The arrested leaders made it clear that they interpreted the ban as an attack upon the Muslim League as a political party. Accused of only dealing with private armies supporting its political adversaries, the Government felt compelled to release the seven leaders on 27th January and to withdraw the ban against the two private armies.[285] In Viceroy Wavell's opinion, Premier Khizar had totally miscalculated the strength of the Muslim League. "The League leaders in the Punjab now think they have got him on the run and will try to secure the downfall of his Government. We may perhaps be in for serious trouble in the Punjab, to add to our other difficulties".[286] One of the Sikhs leaders, Baldev Singh, later complained to the Viceroy that the "very justified" ban had been removed.[287]

At the beginning of February it was reported that even though a Hindu had killed a Muslim during a procession in Lahore, the city remained peaceful and the Muslim League agitation against the Khizar Ministry had so far not resulted in any communal clashes. Nevertheless, the Sikhs perceived the situation as being hostile to them. On 12th February Tara Singh, stated that the purpose of the agitation was the domination of Punjab by Muslims. He called on the Sikhs to prepare themselves to face the Muslim League onslaught

---

285. Ibid.
286. Wavell to Pethick-Lawrence, 29th January 1947, TOP vol. 9, pp.572-575.
287. Baldev Singh to Wavell, 6th February 1947, TOP vol. 9, pp. 626-627.

and to strengthen the Akal Fauj, the Sikh volunteer organisation.[288]

Governor Jenkins also expressed his worries concerning the Muslim League agitation. In his view the leaders of the Muslim League never considered the effect of their communal policy on the minorities, notwithstanding the more liberal views they expressed in private conversations, than what their official policies proclaimed. According to Jenkins it was crucial to reach some kind of political settlement among the three communities and the Government. If a settlement failed, then only one of three options could end the agitation (a) grave communal disturbances, (b) a complete defeat of the League, or (c) a complete defeat of the Ministry.[289] However, the chances of reaching such a political agreement seemed very limited, which intensified an already explosive situation.

Summary

The 1946 provincial election and the political power struggle it triggered off created a new and more severe escalation of violence. The outstanding Muslim League victory came about because the League managed to reach the Muslim electorates by using the religious appeal. However, the Unionists lost their traditional rural support partly because

---

288   FR first half of February 1947, IOL, L/P&J/5/250, p. 75.
289. Governor's letter to the Viceroy dated 15th February 1947, IOL, L/P&J/5/250, p. 86.

of realignment among the landed community and partly because of the drop in agricultural prices since late 1944. In spite of their victory, the political power eluded the League as Unionists could form a new Government in Punjab with support from the Akalis and the Congress. This created a chaotic and turbulent situation, which further minimised the possibility of a peaceful political agreement among the three communities and the political parties. This became manifest in the unprecedented increase in the membership of private armies, which was referred to by officials as 'preparation for war'.

A new characteristic of the violence was deliberate attacks on womenfolk. The violence between Muslims on one side and Sikhs and Hindus on the other was no longer confined to the Mosque, the Temple or the slaughterhouse i.e. the public sphere. It now focused on women as well, i.e. involving the private sphere. This is an important harbinger of the growing genocidal tendency. Even though it wasn't certain in the summer of 1946 that Punjab was heading towards an outbreak of mass violence, the communal groups were becoming thoroughly polarised leaving little space for democratic interaction and peaceful coexistence.

The readiness to wage a civil war became apparent in 1946 when the thousands of casualties took place in Calcutta as a result of the Direct Action Day. Each community was now fully aware that the other was prepared to defend itself and there was no confidence in the Government's ability to enforce law and order. Therefore, private armies were becoming even more belligerent. In a belated attempt to exercise power, the Government decided to ban the RSS and the Muslim League National Guards. But the decision boom ranged as it miscalculated the influence of the private armies and of the Muslim League. Subsequently, the ban had to be lifted three days later. This 'victory' over the Unionist led ministry further fuelled the Muslim agitation, while enhancing the Sikh and Hindu fear. The possibility of reaching a political agreement in the Punjab by early 1947 had almost disappeared.

PART II

THE INTERNECINE STRIFE

Chapter 4
Before and after the Rawalpindi Massacre

From the British Announcement of withdrawal, February 1947 to the Announcement of Partition, June 1947

The political power struggle and the communal relations entered a new phase as Britain expressed preparedness to hand over power to the Indian leadership in the near future. On 20th February 1947, the British, in an attempt to end the political deadlock at the centre and to put pressure on the Indian political leaders, announced that transfer of power would take place no later than 30th June 1948.[290] The announcement made it clear that powers would be handed over "whether as a whole to some form of central Government for British India or in some areas to the existing Provincial Governments".[291] The announcement signified, firstly, that the British were on the verge of departure, secondly, that they would leave irrespective of whether a political agreement between the Congress and the Muslim League was reached or not and thirdly, that a partition of British India was considered an actual possibility.

---

290. Anita Inder Singh, op., cit., p. 212.
291. From the statement of 20th February by the British Government, quoted in Ayesha Jalal, op., cit., p. 237.

The near imminence of such a scenario set in motion a violent power struggle in Punjab. For Jinnah and the League the announcement made it all the more vital to gain control of the political power in Punjab and the statement therefore triggered off a 'Direct Action' campaign against the Khizar Ministry.[292] Consequently, on 24th February huge clashes between the police and the Muslim League were reported at three places, Amritsar, Jullunder and Ambala. The police was forced to shoot at the unruly crowds and there were serious casualties on both sides.[293] An interesting feature in the Muslim League's campaign against the Ministry was the Muslim women's participation in demonstrations, which further bridged the gap between the public and private space.[294]

The Muslim League agitation had a huge impact upon the Sikhs. They felt threatened and Master Tara Singh's initial response was that the Sikhs should revive their army.[295] Furthermore it was declared that they would, if need be, take up arms.[296] As a result, the already troubled relationship between Sikhs and Muslims got even more tense. On 26th February the Muslim agitation was called off and a settlement between the Punjab Government and the

---

292. Anita Inder Singh, op., cit., p. 214.
293. FR second half of February 1947, IOL, L/P&J/5/250, p. 73.
294. David Willmer: "Women as Participants in the Pakistan Movement: Modernization and the Promise of a Moral State", MAS, 30, 3 (1996), pp. 573-590.
295. Swarna Aiyar: Violence and the State in the Partition of Punjab, 1947-48, Cambridge 1994, p.43.
296. FR second half of February 1947, IOL, L/P&J/5/250, p. 73.

Punjab Muslim League was announced amidst doubts as to how long the agreement would last.[297] However, the Governor expressed his clear reservations against the agreement in a letter to the Viceroy: "The real object of the agitation was to turn the Coalition Ministry out of office, and the settlement is therefore unreal because it makes concessions with which the agitation was not really concerned".[298] And only a few days later, on 2nd March, the Khizar Ministry decided to step down. The Muslim League was asked, the following day, to try and form a new Government.

However, the fall of the coalition Government resulted in serious disorder throughout the province. The Sikh leader, Master Tara Singh, had reportedly said "this means war" outside the assembly while swinging his kirpan, and amidst the massive tension, violence soon developed. On 4th March Hindu students began assaulting the police, leaving 30 officers injured with two subsequently dying from their injuries. The sporadic incidents of stabbing and arson soon turned into communal riots in Lahore city.[299] The trouble continued during the night and new riots started on the 5th morning leaving several people dead.[300] The same afternoon, Jenkins again sent a telegram to Viceroy Wavell

297. Governor's letter to the Viceroy dated 28th February 1947, IOL, L/P&J/5/250, p. 80.
298. Ibid.
299. Jenkins to Pethick-Lawrence, 4th March 1947 TOP vol. 9, pp. 850-851.
300. Jenkins to Wavell, telegram 5th March 1947, TOP vol. 9, p. 865.

informing him of the situation in the north-western part of the province. "Multan rioting is reported serious with 20 dead, many injured and many fires. (.).There have been incidents in Rawalpindi likely to lead to rioting. Position in Lahore has deteriorated with many deaths and widespread incendiary incidents. We shall be lucky if we escape rioting throughout Punjab on an unprecedented scale".[301]

By 5th March it was clear that the Muslim League would not be capable of mustering a majority in the provincial Assembly and the Governor decided to proclaim, under section 93 of the Government of India Act, that all responsibility was to be transferred to his office.[302] This enraged the Muslims. For the second time they were left without the political power, and even worse riots took place from 6th March onwards. The riot affected cities were Amritsar, Lahore and Multan and the rural parts of north-western Punjab. Many of the gravest incidents took place in the Rawalpindi Division where the Muslims were in majority. In Rawalpindi and Attock districts especially, casualties seemed to have been heavy.[303] The March rioting witnessed an escalation of violence as never before, which the Governor later described as 'internecine violence' i.e., a mass mutual slaughter among the three communities.[304]

---

301. Jenkins to Wavell, telegram 5th March 1947, TOP vol. 9, pp. 868-870.
302. FR first half of March 1947, IOL, L/P&J/5/250, p. 68.
303. Ibid.
304. Ibid.

The violence, thus, proved to be a curtain raiser to the worst rioting yet to come in August- September.

The fortnightly report blamed both the political parties and the three communities for the carnage. It was mentioned that all communities had made the most of communal disturbances in other parts of India during the year.[305] Even though the Muslim League agitation in January and February 1947 was singled out, the Sikhs and Hindus were not without guilt either. On 3rd March Tara Singh stated that "our motherland is calling for blood and we shall satiate the thirst of our mother with blood".[306] Sikhs declared themselves determined to fight Pakistan and were ready to do anything to prevent the formation of a Muslim League Government and it was reported that Sikhs and Hindus were now strongly in favour of a division of the Punjab.[307] The Congress Working Committee reached a similar conclusion, too. On 8th March the Congress Working Committee published a resolution calling for the partition of Punjab along religious lines.[308]

On 9th March, when the rioting had almost ended, Governor Jenkins sent a letter to the Viceroy with an analysis of the situation. An unusual feature of the riots, according

305. Ibid.
306. Khosla, op., cit., p. 100.
307. FR first half of March 1947, IOL, L/P&J/5/250, p. 68.
308. Resolution the Congress Working Committee on 8th March 1947, Kirpal Singh: Partition of Punjab 1947 , Delhi 1990, pp. 23-24.

to Jenkins, was that firstly, it occurred at two important places at the same time, and secondly, the magnitude. The Sikhs had suffered the most and he emphasised that the Sikh community felt that the Muslim League agitation and the disturbances were a planned attack upon them.[309] Tara Singh had reportedly stated that the "civil war" had already begun and threatened to attack the police stations and organise a Sikh rising.[310] Swarna Aiyar has argued that the riots were organised, which, according to her, points towards an involvement of the private armies.[311] In rural areas especially, attack on villages were conducted following a certain *modus operandi*. A band of outsiders would first surround the village and then approach it, accompanied by beating drums and the shouting of slogans.[312] According to Aiyar, the description of the attacks not only emphasises the level of organisation but also gives the picture of a war-like situation. The violence did not emerge from spontaneous actions of 'the mob' but was instead conducted in an orderly and rational manner. Aiyar also mentions how, in a village near Rawalpindi, white flags were placed on Muslim houses so the attackers could spare them.[313] This kind of deliberate attack on a particular group in a village or town is what genocide scholar Leo Kuper has defined as a "genocidal massacre".[314] In this connection it can be noted that Jenkins,

---

309. Jenkins to Wavell, 9th March 1947, TOP vol. 9, pp. 902-906.
310. Jenkins to Wavell, telegram 10th March 1949, TOP vol. 9, pp. 912-913.
311. Swarna Aiyar, op., cit., p. 50.
312. Ibid., p. 53.
313. Ibid.
314. Leo Kuper op., cit., p. 10.

in the letter on 9th March, for the first time hinted at some possible organisation behind the riots as the violence had started simultaneously at two places.

On 17th March the Governor personally went to the riot affected areas in Attock and Rawalpindi districts to estimate the damage. He noted: "We have already something like 25,000 refugees on our hands from these two districts and Jhelum must cater for 35,000".[315] He further mentioned that the attacks on non-Muslims were organised with extreme savagery.[316] In a letter to the newly appointed Viceroy, Lord Mountbatten, Jenkins wrote that atrocities had taken place especially in the rural areas. He narrated a story of a child in a hospital with both hands cut off and stories of Sikhs being attacked after they had surrendered.

Somehow, Jenkins found it difficult to account for the violence. He mentioned that others like General Messeruy had found indications of organisation and conspiracy behind the riots, but he did not fully agree with this assessment. However, Jenkins pointed out that the Rawalpindi riots had taken place almost simultaneously and that raids in Murree seemed to have been carefully planned and carried out.[317] In his view these riots were caused by "the growth of the Pakistan idea from 1943 onwards, the

---

315. Jenkins to Abell, telegram 17th March 1947, TOP vol. 9, pp. 961-962.
316. Ibid.
317. Jenkins to Wavell, 17th March 1947, TOP vol. 9, pp 965-969.

extreme communalism of the election campaign of 1945-46, the frustration which followed it, the propaganda against the coalition Ministry, the Muslim League agitation, H.M.G's statement of 20th February [of withdrawal], and Khizar's resignation [which] combined touch off an explosive mixture which have been forming for some time".[318]

The full account by General Messeruy was somewhat different. In a note entitled 'Some remarks on the disturbances in the Northern Punjab' , he emphasised that attacks in cities had followed a 'normal pattern', but were fiercer, more sudden and more brutal.[319] What differed from earlier was that rural areas had been affected as well. In some places looting and arson had been the main objective, while in others, killing had been the objective and there were cases where men, women and children had been hacked or beaten to death.[320] There were also instances of forcible conversion of males and abduction of females, along with the burning down of religious shines. Another new feature mentioned by Messeruy was that the violence resulted in a huge number of refugees, especially in Rawalpindi district, where there had also been a "widespread desire to rid many areas of all Sikhs and Hindus, entirely forever. Some former sites of houses have already been ploughed upon". [321] In general the outrages of violence had

318. Ibid.
319. C. Auchinleck to Abell, 22nd March 1947, TOP vol. 9, pp. 1004-1008.
320. Ibid.
321. Ibid.

been of an altogether new nature, which previously would have been totally unexpected. Sexual molestation of women was deliberately used in order to emphasise both the vulnerability of the community and the incapability of the men as protectors. The common social and cultural norms had started breaking down as people no longer perceived a common future together. The many cases of abduction and rape especially, testified to that end. Another feature was that people were forced out of their homes and tens of thousand were rendered refugees overnight. This development marked the beginning of the process of ethnic cleansing along with a widespread desire to get rid of the others 'forever'. This desire emphasised the changes in the nature of violence from traditional violence to genocidal violence.

The burning down of houses and religious places showed that the violence was no longer confined to maintaining a status quo. While destroying people's living places and their place of worship, the violence followed an altogether new rationale. It was now the basic coexistence of Hindus, Sikhs and Muslims, in the Punjab that was under attack. What the perpetrators were out to eradicate was the physical as well as the cultural existence of 'the other'. Thus, the genocidal violence in the Rawalpindi area had a total transformation of the Punjab as its objective. One could thus argue that the massacres turned Punjab into a 'zone of genocide', and a battleground for two opposing and exclusive national discourses.

115

The brutality of the riots made the Viceroy write in his personal report that these massacres were accompanied by sadistic violence which distinguished them from previous ones: "They [the attackers] seem to be very fond of tying whole families together, pouring oil on them and then lighting them as a single torch.[322] This further testified to a clear transformation in the forms of violence. Now whole families including women and children (and not just the men) were turned into targets of violence. Such unheard of cruelty expressed in the riots caused widespread Sikh and Hindu support for a partition of Punjab, more so, since there was no indication of reconciliation among the three communities. The Rawalpindi division was also affected by a large number of refugees, estimated up to 60,000. The administration was also affected by the disturbances as attempts were made to locally reorganise the civil services, police and army on purely communal lines. [323]

A similar picture of mistrust was portrayed in the fortnightly report at the end of March. Never before had the relations between Muslims and non-Muslims been so poor and the possibility for co-operation so remote. The non-Muslims were joining hands on one side and Muslims on the other. Even though the fortnightly report mentioned that the situation had improved and that fewer cases of

---

322. Viceroy's personal report no. 5, TOP vol. 10, pp. 533-547 (paragraph 22).
323. Governor's letter to the Viceroy dated 31st March 1947, IOL, L/P&J/5/250, p. 66.

disorder were reported, it also recognised that this decrease was mainly due to the use of force by the authorities. The feeling of animosity remained intact. The Muslims were even talking of civil war and the tone in public speeches was becoming increasingly belligerent. The Hindus were reportedly helping Sikhs with money and propaganda including the contributions from the Congress Party, which was now accused of communalism and of instigating disorder. "Invisibly but definitely all non-Muslims have been drawn together and there has been a manifest stiffening in their resolve neither to collaborate with the Muslims nor to suffer their domination. Even Muslim Congressmen are dismayed for they feel that their parent body has discarded its pretence of nationalism and they are anxiously considering where their loyalty should be given". [324]

The riots that took place in the beginning of the March caused an unprecedented number of casualties. According to the first official estimates 2090 were killed and 1142 were seriously injured. The Sikhs, especially, had suffered heavy loses and the feeling of being unprepared had bitten deep into their pride combined with desire for retaliation. "The important question about the Sikhs is not if and when they intend to fight. It is whether, if the Sikh leaders continue as they are doing, they will be able to hold

---

324. FR second half of March 1947, IOL, L/P&J/5/250, p. 60.

their following in check and maintain their discipline".[325] Later on the number of estimated victims of the March riots increased while the official but incomplete estimates were 3.000 killed and 1.200 seriously injured.[326] The fact that the number of killed had more than doubled the number of injured emphasises the genocidal intent of the perpetrators.

Many former soldiers from the Indian British army had returned back after the second world war only to find unemployment. The private armies filled this vacuum and offered them stability in the fast changing political environment. These out of work soldiers provided professional expertise to the amateur groups. This military connection is further emphasised with the army style organisational set-up and the frequent use of military weaponry.[327] The membership of community armies also increased significantly during March. According to British officials the RSS membership reached 50,400 and the Muslim League National Guards 38,467 and both were very anxious to arm their volunteers. One of the Sikh bodies, the Akal Saina, had in March alone obtained 4,600 new members and a total membership of 6,600. They were along with the other Akali regiments expected to join arms with the RSS against the Muslims. "The unity prevailing between the two communities on the subject of an anti-Muslim front

---

325. Ibid.
326. Ibid.
327. Swarna Aiyar, op., cit., p. 67.

is now virtually complete and the two volunteer organisations can be expected to act as one".[328] This development showed how the private armies were extending their presence and their legitimacy as defenders of the communities. The Rawalpindi massacre had psychologically resulted in people aligning themselves, to an even larger extent, along communal lines. The entrance of the violence into the private arena made it even more impossible for people to avoid getting involved in the fighting. Now they risked being attacked only because of their religious affiliation. This development further led to an even stronger community alignment.

The tense situation continued in April where clashes took place in several districts. Amritsar city and the district of Gurgaon were particularly affected by both arson and stabbing.[329] Nevertheless, many Punjabis hoped that the ongoing negotiations in Delhi would bring about a durable result acceptable to everybody. The negotiations were of vital importance, particularly to the Sikhs and they were eager to ensure that the Punjab did not end as a pawn in the All-India game. The continued tension combined with Sikh fear concerning the negotiations further fuelled the Sikh agitation that was kept alive by two documents circulating within the Sikh community. The first one was a leaflet exaggerating the number of victims during the March

328. FR second half of March 1947, IOL, L/P&J/5/250, p. 59.
329. FR first half of April 1947, IOL, L/P&J/5/250, p. 58.

riots. The second one, according to Jenkins, appeared to be an appeal to contribute to a war fund.[330] Even though both documents could be read as legitimate cries for help they could also be interpreted as preliminary indications of violent action against the Muslims. The latter interpretation was also supported by intelligence reports of the activities of Tara Singh and Kartar Singh.[331] At a meeting held in Delhi on 14th April about the prospects of division of Punjab, Governor Jenkins was asked for the alternatives to partition. He stated reversion of the Unionist Party, partition or civil war as possible alternatives. If neither a revival of the Unionist Party nor partition proved durable, there would be no option except (British) departure and then leaving it to the communities to fight it out.[332] He concluded that the Sikhs would definitely want to fight at some point, but would probably prefer to wait until the British had left.

Throughout April, arson and stabbing continued in many places and even experimental bomb making was reported. A joint appeal from Gandhi and Jinnah had no effect on the communal bitterness that appeared even deeper.[333] This cleavage was also reflected in the increasing activities of the volunteer organisations. A new Sikh corps had been formed at Amritsar, and the Muslims had increased

---

330. Jenkins to Mountbatten, 9th April 1947, TOP vol. 10, pp. 172-173.
331. Ibid.
332. Meeting between, Ismay, Caroe, Jenkins, Mieville, Wieghtman, Abell and Capt. Lascelles on 14th April 1947, TOP vol. 9, pp. 231-234.
333. FR second half of April 1947, IOL, L/P&J/5/250, p. 51.

their number of volunteers as reportedly another 5,630 youth had joined the Muslim League National Guards. [334]

At the same time, the difficulties in reaching an agreement in Delhi became more and more apparent. The Sikhs found the negotiations problematic as they were not only bitterly opposed to Pakistan but were also displeased at the prospect of being swallowed by 'Hindustan'. But most of all they were afraid of being attacked once again and the report mentioned that "the Sikh propaganda machine is increasing in efficiency and is doing much to keep the Sikh temper inflamed". [335] In Lahore city, Muslims were conducting a campaign to burn out non-Muslims from the beginning of April and in mid-July the number of burned out houses exceeded 700. According to Governor Jenkins, there was evidence that the arsonists had been paid. [336]

From the beginning of May and onwards the number of communal clashes multiplied. In May, the combined death toll for 1947 had already reached 3300 in addition to 1400 seriously injured. [337] On several occasions the Governor had to impose curfew in anticipation of violence. [338] At the same time the disturbances continued and the number of casualties piled up. Between 13th and 15th May, 12 to 15

---

334. Ibid.
335. Ibid.
336. Ian Talbot: Punjab and the Raj, 1849-1947, op., cit., p. 229.
337. FR first half of May 1947, IOL, L/P&J/5/250, p. 43.
338. Governor's letter to the Viceroy dated 15th May 1947, IOL, L/P&J/5/250, p. 49.

people were reportedly killed in Lahore alone and the Governor did not see any sign of improvement. Outside Lahore and Amritsar there was tension almost everywhere and a fairly large number of crude weapons were recovered.[339] So far none among the Muslim League National Guards, the RSS or the Akali regiments were expected to have amassed any modern weapons.

However, the Sikhs fears of a political oblivion were far from allayed as the negotiations with the British and the political parties bore no results. Instead the fear of communal violence loomed larger than ever before. On 19th May Jenkins had a discussion about partition with Tara Singh, who made it clear that no solution could be reached between the Sikhs and the Muslims since neither community would submit to communal domination.[340] According to him the Muslims would massacre all Sikhs and Hindus placed in Pakistan and in retaliation all Muslims would be massacred in the Indian part of Punjab.

The prospect of mass violence was amply supported by an intelligence report too. According to the report the Sikhs were determined to strike against Muslims. First, in the areas where the non-Muslims already constituted a majority, secondly, in areas that they were demanding in

---

339. Ibid., p. 48.
340. Note by Jenkins, 19th May 1947, TOP vol. 10, pp. 893-894.

case of partition, and thirdly, the violence would also be directed against the Punjab Police Force. Even though the intelligence report found the organisational level to be incomplete, the Sikh leaders were doing their best to prepare their followers for something big in the near future.[341] Thus, they were, to some extent, given a de facto approval from their communal leadership. Furthermore, Sikhs were allegedly supported financially by big Hindu businessmen, besides receiving support from most of the Sikh princely States. "Patiala (Maharaja) is said to have agreed to supply arms and ammunition as well as explosive. He is supposed to have sent some of his soldiers, armed and in mufti [civilian clothes], already to Amritsar".[342]

The tense and belligerent atmosphere persisted through the second half of May, where a considerable deterioration in the communal situation was reported. "In Amritsar [since] 11th April]. (.). more than four hundred and sixty persons have either been killed or injured". And since 9th May there have been three hundred and twenty-five victims of communal strife [in Lahore]".[343] Even though the pattern of violence differed somewhat, with stabbing incidents defining the violence in Lahore and the crude bomb explosions being located mainly in Amritsar, there remained several obvious similarities. For instance, arson was used

---

341. Abbott to Capt. Brockman, 21st May 1947, TOP vol. 10, p. 942.
342. Ibid.
343. FR second half of May 1947, IOL, L/P&J/5/250, p. 36.

at both places and the violence showed signs of better organisation combined with a greater determination of the perpetrators. [344]

Around this time, other parts of the Punjab were also engulfed in the communal disturbances and in nearly every district there were cases of bomb explosions, arson and communal killings. On 25th May, in Gurgaon district, Hindus attacked a Muslim village. The Muslims later retaliated and the entire district was more or less consumed by communal warfare. According to estimates, fifty villages were heavily affected by the violence and a large number of people were either killed or wounded. To emphasise the seriousness of the situation the fortnightly report mentioned that: "An indication of the widespread and serious character of the situation is contained in a report which states that in one day the military and police fired as many as a thousand rounds". [345]

Predictably, the recruitment and the armament of the private armies continued unabated during this period. The RSS now had an estimated membership of 56,800 and was reportedly involved in bomb making and even suspected of being instrumental in igniting the riots in Gurgaon. The Muslim League National Guards were also very active in arming their community. The Sikh army, the

---

344. Ibid.
345. Ibid.

Akal Fauj had also attracted a considerable strength of estimated 8,500 members, while another Sikh body, the *Shahidi Jathas* (suicide squad) was successfully appealing to many in the community. It was reported that there was a *Jatha* (Sikh army band) in almost every Sikh village in Lyallpur and Sheikhupura districts in central Punjab. However, since they were spread out over a large area and organised locally, their precise number was unknown but was assumed to make a big figure.[346]

The peak of summer with temperatures as high as 112-116 F degree was also reported to have affected the public behaviour in a more aggressive way. At the same time, an already overworked police force was not only suffering the heat, but also abuses for doing their job. The communal sentiments and awareness were furthermore growing in the services, making law enforcement even more difficult.[347]

Summary

During the period from February to June 1947 the conflict in the Punjab reached a new level. This period is characterised by the unprecedented degree of violence by all three communities. It was not just that the brutality of the violence deepened, the number of perpetrators and victims also expanded manifold. Victims also included women and children, who were drawn more and more into

---

346. Ibid., p. 35.
347. Ibid.

the communal conflict. The British announcement of complete withdrawal, on 20th February, prompted the Muslim League to renew its attack on the Khizar Government. The agitation succeeded in bringing the Government down. However, being unable to guarantee a majority in the assembly the Muslim League was not allowed to form a new Government. Instead the Governor used his power under the constitution to declare Governor's rule in the province. This was followed by severe communal unrest. Both the Sikhs and Hindus were agitated by the fall of the Ministry and consequently, riots started in the two main cities of the Punjab - Lahore and Amritsar. The rioting in rural areas of the north-western Punjab, however, exceeded the violence in the urban parts of the province. An unprecedented number of people were killed and injured in a civil war like rioting. Though the main perpetrators were Muslims and the main victims Sikhs, the Governor baptised correctly the violence as part of an 'internecine strife'.

The days of rioting in March left the Punjab more divided than ever before. The first call for a partition of the province was made by the Congress Working Committee and subsequently backed by Hindus and Sikhs. The Sikh community was engulfed with bitterness because of the March rioting and expressed fear of being caught unprepared once again. All three communities continued arming themselves and the membership of the private armies also increased. Furthermore, the tone in the press became more and more belligerent and uncompromising.

126

The violence, which previously had been localised, and somewhat limited was now liberated and brutalised. The character of the violence had changed and the mutuality of the feud disappeared as the main target became the private sphere. The rationale of the violence was no longer a question of maintaining status quo but of ethnically cleansing one's area. The perpetrators of the violence appeared to have been better organised than during earlier riots. The new location and the brutality of the violence showed a willingness to commit both ethnic cleansing and genocidal violence. There was a total breakdown of the cultural order and taboos were therefore, violated. The violence differed from the traditional violence by its magnitude, brutality and by making it almost impossible for people to continue living together. This was especially true in the case of refugees, as no earlier riots had caused people to permanently leave their homes on a massive scale.

In the main cities, especially Lahore and Amritsar, arson and stabbing persisted throughout April and May and in the rural areas, the number of organised raids against villages increased. Governor Jenkins found an agreeable partition a virtual impossibility. By the time the summer hit Punjab in May 1947, the conflict had already reached the boiling point.

Chapter 5
Partition and Transfer of Power

From June till 15ᵗʰ August 1947

The announcement of British withdrawal heralded a series of consultations between British and Indian leaders. During the negotiations it became apparent to the Viceroy, Lord Mountbatten, that reaching a settlement based on the framework of the Cabinet Mission Plan was impossible.[348] Thereby unable to reach a political agreement but determined to leave, a plan for partition and a transfer of power to two states, India and Pakistan, was put forward by the British. On 3ʳᵈ June the partition plan was announced with a transfer of power as early as 15ᵗʰ August.[349] According to the plan the decision to partition Punjab and Bengal should be taken by their legislative assemblies. The Muslim and non-Muslim members were supposed to vote separately and if a simple majority of either part decides in favour of partition "division will take place" and arrangements "made accordingly".[350]

---

348. Viceroy Mountbatten's Broadcast on the All-India Radio, 3rd June 1947, in Kirpal Singh: Partition of Punjab 1947 , New Delhi 1991, p. 91. For an description of the negotiations see: Ayesha Jalal, op., cit., pp. 241-293.
349. Anita Inder Singh, op. cit., p. 232.
350. Statement by His Majesty's Government. Dated the 3rd June 1947, in Kirpal Singh, op., cit., p. 94.

For the administration partition would mean that all assets, liabilities, police, courts etc. would be divided.[351]

In the Punjab, the plan was received with mixed feelings. It was neither rejected up front nor met with ready acceptance either.[352] In some districts where it was accepted, it diminished the levels of tension, while flaring up tension in other areas. The internecine violence continued engulfing territories and devouring new victims. Pakistan was now almost a reality but the crucial question was how the subsequent partition of Punjab (and Bengal) was going to take place. The Sikhs especially reacted strongly against the partition plan because of fear that it would divide them and reduce them to minorities in both an Indian and a Pakistani Punjab.[353] The *Shrimoni Akali Dal,* a Sikh political party, therefore, issued a circular calling Pakistan 'a death to the Sikhs' and declared that Sikhs wanted a free sovereign state with the Chenab and the Jamna rivers as its borders.[354]

This gave a fresh lease of life to the ongoing violence. On 4th June, five deaths and five fires were reported from Lahore alone, and Amritsar witnessed two communal riots and four fires, leaving four people killed and nine injured. The Gurgaon district was still in disorder and an estimated

---

351. Ibid., p. 97.
352. FR first half of June 1947 IOL, L/P&J/5/250, p. 29.
353. Ibid.
354. Ibid.

60 villages were more or less burned down. The number of exact casualties was unknown, but acknowledged numbers of deaths was over 100.[355] On 7th June, Jenkins again reported disturbances in Lahore and Amritsar and he described the general situation as unchanged and unsatisfactory.[356] The Hindus in the west and Muslims in the east were dissatisfied with the prospect of partition, and the Sikhs now pinned their faith on the Boundary Commission that had the task of drawing a new borderline.

The fortnightly report from the first half of June tried to analyse why the fighting in Lahore and Amritsar had been so severe. One of the reasons it emphasised upon was, that the right to possess Punjab's two principal cities was disputed and secondly, that the masses realised that despite a measure of agreement to compromise at the centre, there was no improvement in the relations between the communities and no lessening in the estrangement which persisted among the provincial leaders.[357] The Gurgaon district was so badly affected by the communal riots, that it was described as amounting to a primitive war.[358] In a nutshell, it was the right to define and possess the Punjab that was at stake.

355. Jenkins to Mountbatten, telegram 4th June 1947, TOP vol. 11, p. 136.
356. Jenkins to Mountbatten, telegram 7th June 1947, TOP vol. 11, p. 194-195.
357. FR first half of June 1947 IOL, L/P&J/5/250, p. 29.
358. Governor's letter to the Viceroy dated 15th June 1947 IOL, L/P&J/5/250, p. 34.

The decision to partition Punjab (and Bengal) was endorsed by the Congress Working Committee on June 14. In his speech at the meeting Gandhi expressed his reluctant acceptance of the decision emphasising his profound sadness the turn of events. In an almost prophetic manner he ended his address saying. "This decision put both our religions on trail. The world is watching us. In the three-quarters of the country that has fallen in our share, Hinduism is going to be tested. If you show the generosity of true Hinduism, you will rise in the eyes of the world. If not, you will have proved Mr. Jinnah's thesis that Muslims and Hindus are two separate nations, that Hindus forever will be Hindus and Muslims forever Muslims, that the two will never unite, and that the Gods of the two are different".[359]

And while Hinduism awaited being tested the overall number of casualties in the province since the end of 1946 rather testified towards a state of war. From 18th November 1946 to 15th May 1947 reportedly 3280 were killed and 1390 injured. The actual numbers was assumed to be even higher since figures from Rawalpindi and Gurgaon districts were still uncertain.[360] Both Jinnah and Nehru were reportedly very concerned about the magnitude of the violence and Nehru even suggested imposing martial law.[361]

---

359. Gandhi's address at the Congress Working Committee meeting on June 14, in H.D. Sharma, op. cit., p. 384.
360. Abbott to Abell, telegram 15th June 1947, TOP vol. 11, p. 397.
361. Mountbatten to Jenkins, telegram 24th June 1947, TOP vol. 11, p. 594.

Jenkins, however, found that martial law wasn't the solution to this kind of trouble, which he did not define as rioting, but as 'cloak and dagger'[362] activities. He suggested that the "real remedy is active intervention by political leaders not by Press statements but by contacts which they unquestionably possess with violent elements. Muslim League in my opinion started burning and stabbing and Hindu bombing is the work of RSS".[363] But his suggestions were not even considered and bomb attacks got even more frequent and efficient.

Between 15th and 21st June six cases of bomb attacks were reported and about 17 people (mostly Muslims) were killed and 118 injured (again mainly Muslims), all cases testifying to a high level of organisation behind the violence. On 15th a bomb exploded in a drain in a private hospital. When the police arrived and a large group had gathered, another bomb was thrown killing one and wounding 43. The following day (16th), 2 Muslims were killed and five received injuries, after a bomb was thrown at them. The culprit was believed to be a Sikh. The night between the 16th and 17th a bomb was thrown on the roof of a Muslim house where several people were sleeping, four were killed and five were injured. On 19th morning a bomb was thrown at a group of Muslim workers, leaving one killed and injuring

---

362. Jenkins to Mountbatten, telegram 24th June 1947, TOP vol. 11, pp. 605-606.
363. Ibid.

11. On 20th a bomb exploded in a truck carrying Hindu labourers, it was still unknown whether the truck had been attacked or whether one of the workers had the bomb with him. 16 received injuries in the incident. Finally, on 21st, two bombs were thrown in Sabzi Mandi killing nine and leaving 38 injured.[364]

It was the Governor's understanding that the political parties were aware of what was going on and that within the Party organisations there were people who controlled the perpetrators and supplied the money.[365] This interpretation further emphasised the level of organisation in the violence and more importantly a certain degree of intent. Even though there was no clear evidence that the political leaders were directly involved, the parties were *de facto* providing people with 'a license to kill' through aiding and abetting.

The decision to partition the Punjab received its 'democratic' blueprint on 23rd June when the voting took place. While the Muslim members of the assembly voted against partition the non-Muslim voted in favour.[366] Partition was thereby becoming an undisputed reality. At the same time, the private armies were becoming more influential as a greater number of people were volunteering to each of

364. Jenkins to Mountbatten, 25th June 1947, TOP vol. 11, pp. 623-628.
365. Ibid.
366. Ayesha Jalal, op., cit., p. 290. An identical result was reached in Bengal on 20th June

them. The RSS had accumulated an estimated membership of 59,200. The Muslim League National Guards total number had gone up to estimated 42,300. And the various Sikh bodies, after the merger of Akal Fauj and Shahidi Jathas, constituted a number of at least 8,000.[367] On the whole, around 110,000 people were organised in some sort of military structure. Therefore, Punjab remained tense and it was considered unlikely that a real peace agreement could be reached, even though June witnessed a temporary ceasefire due to a joint peace appeal. The fighting, however, remerged and clashes were reported from Gurgaon, Gurdaspur, Gurjanwala and Jullunder districts, and the principal cities Lahore and Amritsar. The Punjab now had the unique description of being a powder keg, where "the danger is constant that despite the peace appeals, some sparks will set the whole pile ablaze".[368]

A joint appeal peace did help improve the communal relations in Amritsar and Lahore during the beginning of July, but there were further disturbances in Gurjanwala city and in the rural areas of Amritsar district. The people were reportedly still unsure whether it would be safe to stay after the partition or not.[369] Another uncertainty was the division line. After an interview Jenkins had with one of the Sikh

---

367. FR second half of June 1947 IOL, L/P&J/5/250, p. 21.
368. Ibid.
369. FR first half of July 1947 IOL, L/P&J/5/250, p. 14. (This is the last of the Fortnightly Reports kept in the British files).

leaders, Giani Kartar Singh, he reported that Giani Kartar Singh had been extremely frank about the intentions of the Sikhs.[370] There would be trouble, if they did not like the decision of the Boundary Commission and that they would accept nothing short of Chenab river as the western boundary. The Muslims, however, were hoping to reach as far as Ambala division and the Governor felt that "everyone [was] behaving as though they had just been at war and were going to have a new war within a few weeks".[371]

To add to the confusion, the very difficult assignment of drawing the boundary was entrusted to a British official Sir Cyril Radcliff, who, without having any connection to India or Indian politics, was given the crucial task of partitioning India in the Bengal and Punjab provinces. His only guidelines were to draw the boundary according to religious affiliation even though other factors could be taken into consideration.[372] He arrived in Delhi on 8th July for the first time and had only little more than five weeks to make the boundary.[373] Therefore, not surprisingly, there was little hope for a peaceful solution. The most conspicuous problem mentioned by the Governor was whether an agreement on

370. Jenkins to Mountbatten, 10th July 1947, TOP vol. 12, pp. 71-74.
371. Ibid.
372. Tan Tai Young: "Sir Cyril Goes to India: Partition, Boundary-Making and Disruptions in the Punjab", in International Journal of Punjab Studies, vol. 4, 1 (1997), pp. 1-20.
373. Ishtiaq Ahmed: "The 1947 Partition of Punjab: Arguments put Forth before the Punjab Boundary Commission by the Parties involved", in Ian Talbot and Gurharpal Sing (eds.): Region and Partition. Bengal, Punjab and the Partition of the Subcontinent", Karachi 1999, p. 122.

the boundary line would be reached at all. According to Jenkins it was likely that the actual transfer of power would be accompanied by disorders, but he found it impossible to predict whether it would break out before or after 15th August.[374] He expected the Sikhs to create problems since it was highly unlikely that they would approve of any boundary. And to make the matters worse, the monsoon had been delayed and the central and western Punjab was left hot and dry.[375]

To counter the anxiety concerning the partition, on 24th July it was announced by the Partition Council[376] that both India and Pakistan would guarantee protection to all their citizens and that they had agreed to set up a special military command, the Punjab Boundary Force, from 1st August covering the civil districts of Sialkot, Gujranwala, Sheikhupura, Lyallpur, Montgomery, Lahore, Amritsar, Gurdaspur, Hoshiarpur, Jullundur, Ferozepore and Ludhiana.[377] It was further announced that British General-Major T.W. Rees was going to lead the force, while Brigadier Digamber Singh from India and Colonel Ayub Khan from Pakistan were going to be second in command.

374. Jenkins to Mountbatten, 10th July 1947, TOP vol. 12, pp. 71-74.
375. Ibid.
376. The Council, which was constituted on 27th June, consisted of, Viceroy Mountbatten, Muslim League leader Muhammad Ali Jinnah, Liaqat Ali Khan (Muslim League), and Sardar Vallabhbhai Patel and Rajendra Prasad, both from the Congress Party.
377. Mounbatten to Listowel, telegram 24th July 1947, TOP vol. 12, pp. 326-327.

Notwithstanding the assurances to the minorities, Sikhs from western Punjab were again on the move and all communities appeared ready to make an exodus. The second half of July was overshadowed by speculations with regard to the Boundary Commission's award. The July report expressed concern that the Sikh community appeared to be preparing for a potential showdown with the Muslims. The strength of the Jathas was now estimated to be around 19,000 and both arson and bomb attacks continued unabated.[378] Between 19th and 22nd July, six serious bomb explosions occurred in Lahore city and from villages in Lahore district there were reports of violence. There was a growing risk that the fighting might spread to other parts of central Punjab. In Ferozepore district several incidents had already been reported.[379] The rural areas of Amritsar were also affected by rioting wherein Muslims had been killed and, according to the Governor, Sikhs were the prime aggressors. Bombs were now being widely used and many more people seemed to be in possession of firearms.

The implementation of the partition plan, i.e. dividing assets, liabilities etc., was going very slowly and Governor Jenkins did not detect any enthusiasm for partition per se. The Muslims appeared pleased with the creation of Pakistan, but as Punjabis they wanted the whole of Punjab.

---

378. FR second half of July, in Kirpal Singh, op., cit., p. 302.
379. Governor's letter to the Viceroy dated 30th July 1947, IOL, L/P&J/5/250, p. 11.

"It would be difficult enough to partition within six weeks a country of 30 million people which has been governed as a unit for 98 years, even if all concerned were friendly and anxious to make progress".[380] Jenkins reported that the migration of Muslims to the west and Non-Muslims to the east continued. It was his belief that when the transfer of power had taken place there would hardly be any Muslim officials left in east Punjab where 33 per cent were Muslims, or Hindu/Sikh officials in the west where 27 per cent were non-Muslims.

In addition to his report, minutes of a meeting between him and Giani Kartar Singh were enclosed. Giani Kartar Singh had brought to his attention the importance of integrity of the Sikh community and demanded (a) an exchange of population as to bring Sikhs into East Punjab and (b) to claim Nankana Sahib (birthplace of guru Nanak, the first guru) and other historical Gurudwaras (Sikh temples). The Governor had replied that the Sikhs only had themselves to thank for what was going to happen. They shouldn't have called for a partition in the first place with such a sparse population. The Governor informed him that it was now too late to change anything and the Sikh community had no choice but to accept the award. The Governor also informed Giani Kartar Singh that Jinnah had guaranteed religious and personal freedom to the minorities in Pakistan.

---

380. Ibid., p. 10.

Giani Kartar Singh replied that he had no confidence in Jinnah and that the Sikhs were in great danger. Therefore, he refused to be part of a joint statement that promised no disturbances when the award was announced.[381] The Governor repeatedly emphasised that the Sikh community had to accept the award in the end and that all demonstrations against it would be futile. He also rejected the Sikhs dissatisfaction and said that partition would not be as bad as they thought.

"Finally, the Giani Sahib burst into tears, as at our last interview, and said that it was my duty to protect his small and oppressed community".[382] The appeal by Giani Kartar Singh aptly sums up the Sikh desperation. These minutes very clearly betray the growing fears and insecurity among the Sikh community. The prospect of their ancestral land being partitioned coupled with the uncertain status that they would have in a new Pakistan or India were the realities confronting the community. The violence almost seemed to be the last resort. According to a telephone conversation between Abbott and Abell (private secretary to the Viceroy) on 1st August, the trouble with the Sikhs seemed inevitable. The raids on Muslim villages had already begun. Even the trains had been attacked or attempts made

---

381. Minute on Governor's meeting on 30th July 1947 at 3.30 pm with Giana Kartar Singh, IOL, L/P&J/5/250, p. 13.
382. Ibid., p. 12.

to attack during the last couple of days. Since the night of 30th/31st July, 23 people had been killed and 30 wounded in Amritsar district alone.[383]

The suspicions of involvement of Sikh leaders became clearer in the beginning of August and Master Tara Singh was the prime suspect. The crucial question for the Governor was whether to arrest him right away or give it a chance.[384] During a meeting on 5th August a more substantial account for the accusations against Tara Singh was put forward. Captain Savage from the police force narrated a statement by a man called Pritam Singh who had been arrested for instigating riots. According to the statement Master Tara Singh was involved both in the production of bombs and in planning attacks.[385] A statement of another arrested person called Gopal Rai Khosla supported the accusations against Tara Singh. "He had seen Tara Singh towards the end of July and had asked for 700 rupees outstanding for the purchase of rifles and grenades already promised by Tara Singh".[386] Tara Singh had mentioned that four or five Sikhs were planning to blow up "the Pakistan Special [train transporting staff between Delhi and Karachi] with remote control firing apparatus and after wrecking the Special, to

---

383. Telephone message from Abbott to Abell, 1st August 1947, TOP vol. 12, p. 459.
384. Jenkins to Abell, 4th August 1947, TOP vol. 12, p. 527.
385. Record of interview between Mountbatten, Jinnah, Ali Khan, Sardar Patel and Capt. Savage, 5th August 1947, TOP vol. 12, pp. 537-539.
386. Ibid.

set it on fire, and shoot the occupants".[387]

During the meeting it was debated whether Tara Singh should be arrested immediately and whether such action would result in trouble in the central Punjab. Mountbatten decided to recommend to Governor Jenkins that Master Tara Singh should be arrested when the Boundary Commission award was made public.[388] In a subsequent letter to Jenkins, he stressed that while he should have time to consider the conclusions of the meeting, it was none the less "definitely the view of the meeting that a) the arrest should be made, and b) that they should not be made for a week or so".[389] Nevertheless on 8th August Mountbatten made it clear that he considered Jenkins to be the most competent judge in this situation. He also agreed to wait and see the reactions to the award before making any arrest, if so desired by the Governor.[390]

The very same day Jenkins sent a telegram to the Viceroy to inform him of the seriousness of the situation. The daily casualties were estimated between 50-100 and the Commander of the newly established Punjab Boundary Force had informed him that the "strength of his 5 Brigade groups average 1500 effective rifles. This means that in addition to police we have a strength of say 7500 effective

387. Ibid.
388. Ibid.
389. Abell to Jenkins, 5th August 1947, TOP vol. 12, p. 539.
390. Mountbatten to Jenkins, telegram 8th August 1947, TOP vol. 12, pp. 580-581.

rifles to control 12 districts with a population of no less than 12 millions".[391] As for the decision to arrest Tara Singh and others, Jenkins along with the new Governors of east and west Punjab, Sir C. M. Trivedi and Sir Francis Mudie respectively, was of the opinion that it would rather worsen than improve the situation. Jenkins felt that it would be better if this matter was left to be dealt with by the new Governments of east and west Punjab.[392] And thereby avoiding the British to become party to a violent battle weeks before their exit. To endorse his views further, he wrote that the ongoing raids of villages were not specifically controlled by Tara Singh and others, but an outcome of their general propaganda. As a precautionary measure, he could arrange for their arrest but emphasised that it would be difficult since the Sikh leaders were mostly staying at the Golden Temple. In remark to this telegram, Mountbatten wrote that he approved Jenkins decision, and emphasised that until 15th August, it was his business, and there was no reason to tell Jinnah: "If asked I shall say - 'I left it to Jenkins to decide when'. If he decides 'after 15th' that is his concern".[393] The same willingness to postpone the matter was also exercised in connection with the publication of the Punjab Boundary Award. Though the award was ready for publication by 9th evening, the announcement was withheld to avoid British responsibility for the riots, which

---

391. Jenkins to Mountbatten, telegram 8th August 1947, TOP vol. 12, pp. 583-584.
392. Jenkins to Mountbatten, telegram 9th august 1947, TOP vol. 12, pp. 636-637.
393. Ibid.

"undoubtedly" would follow.[394] On 12th August, Mountbatten informed Jenkins that the award for Punjab wouldn't be ready before 15th evening or 16th morning[395] and therefore not available until after independence itself.

The uncertainty about the Boundary award made the violence almost inevitable. While the people in the disputed areas were unsure of where to go and when, the authorities seemed quite reluctant to enforce law and order. It looked like there was no blueprint for containing the large-scale violence that the British officers had anticipated all along. Even though one should exercise caution while arguing that the British aided and abetted the violence, it is nevertheless certain that the inconsistent and hesitant way of handling the very virulent situation did send an unambiguous signal to the perpetrators that law and order was highly unlikely to be enforced. The insufficient strength of the Boundary Force combined with the disregard of the Governor's various warnings further proves that the British either didn't have the sufficient force to counter the violence or simply didn't want to sacrifice its soldiers.

On the evening on 9th August the first fully organised

394. Extract From the Viceroy's 69th Staff Meeting on 9th August 1947, in Kirpal Singh op., cit., pp. 458-459.
395. Mountbatten to Jenkins, telegram 12th August 1947, TOP vol. 12, p. 687. In a telegram on 13th August to Governor Burrows in Bengal and Governor Jenkins in Punjab, Mounbatten writes that the Boundary Commission award not will be published before 16th August; Mountbatten to Burrows and Jenkins, telegram 13th August 1947, TOP vol. 12, p. 693.

train attack took place. A 'Pakistan Special'[396] train was derailed after hitting a mine in the eastern Punjab (near Amritsar), leaving one women and one child dead, while 10 persons were slightly injured.[397] The culprits had disappeared into the Sikh State of Faridkot in a jeep. The law and order situation had virtually broken down. This was especially true in the eastern part where there were hardly any police officers left since Muslims constituted around 90% of the Punjab police force.[398] Moreover, the disarming of Muslim policemen in Amritsar, made officers and their families fear for their safety and many had already started leaving. Punjab was on the verge of surrender to chaos and violence. The disturbances were producing an average daily killing of about 100 people with occasional raids in which 70-80 people were killed in one full swoop.[399] These bigger raids were more organised and carried out by well-armed and well-led groups.[400]

While the situation in Amritsar and Lahore further deteriorated, the police force became more unreliable and the private armies more active.[401] The raids and murders were now happening so frequently that it was difficult to

---

396. Transporting Muslim officials and their families.
397. Abell to Governor Secretary Sind, telegram 10th August 1947, TOP vol. 12, p. 648.
398. Swarna Aiyar, op., cit., p. 68.
399. Note by Major General D.C. Hawthorn, 11th August 1947, TOP vol. 12, pp. 667-668.
400. Ibid.
401. Jenkins to Mountbatten, telegram 12th August 1947, TOP vol. 12, p. 688.

keep track of them all and reports on the situation were most likely incomplete.[402] Both urban and rural areas of Punjab seemed infected. Many trains had been attacked and even groups of refugees were attacked and butchered. The fighting had now spread to almost all parts of the province. The attacks on trains and on refugee convoys conducted with military precision made it evident that the violence was organised. The attacks on people who had already been forced to migrate highlighted the genocidal intent. They were massacred in order to prevent their return.

According to Jenkins description, the Sikhs were responsible for most of the killing in rural areas. "Most of the rural casualties - and they have been heavy - have been caused by Sikhs working in fairly large bands and raiding Muslim villages or Muslim pockets in mixed villages".[403] However, from time to time, Muslims hit back. In Jelalabad village in the Lahore district around 70 Hindus had been killed. The cities were not spared either from the growing inferno. In Lahore, the tension went to the boil when a huge number of refugees arrived from Amritsar telling not only about their own sufferings but also about Muslim police officers being disarmed. On 11th and 12th the situation exploded causing more than 100 casualties and as many as 50 fires. Only non-Muslim properties were affected and the

---

402. Governor's letter to the Viceroy dated 13th August 1947, IOL, L/P&J/5/250, p. 7.
403. Ibid.

police, reportedly, for the first time showed open indiscipline. They seemed more concerned with the fate of their fellow Muslims in Amritsar than with the fate of non-Muslims in Lahore. Some policemen even took part in "looting houses". When about 15 Sikhs were killed in a Gurudwara in Lahore city on 11th August, the Inspector General reported that the police almost certainly "connived at", if not actually carried out, "this massacre".[404]

In light of the continuous violence and the growing indiscipline in the police force the biggest problem was the risk of mass violence and forced migration. The Governor wrote that it would be extremely difficult for the Punjab Boundary Force and its commander to keep in control those twelve districts, which were to be divided. The number of affected people was estimated at 12 million, distributed over 17,932 inhabited towns and villages and estimates suggested that as many as 20,000 well trained men would be needed. Unfortunately the effective strength of the Punjab Boundary Force was only about 7,500. (Cf. above).

On August 11 Jinnah delivered his first speech to the Constituent Assembly of Pakistan in Karachi thanking the members for electing him as President. Against the background of massive violence already perpetrated in Punjab, either in the name of Hindustan Zindabad or Pakistan Zindabad, the address appeared somewhat

404. Ibid., p. 6.

147

misplaced. Seven years after having argued the necessity of a separate homeland for Muslims, Jinnah, on the eve of Pakistan's independence, appealed to Hindus and Muslims to work together. The surprise was not the appeal in itself, but the emphasis, "that in the course of time the Hindus would cease to be Hindus and Muslims would cease to be Muslims, not in the religious sense, because that is the personal faith of each individual, but in the political sense as citizens of the state".[405] But by then it was too late. The logic of the two-nation theory had already captivated the mindset of people. Many historians have been puzzled by Jinnah's speech and have found it difficult to understand. Some have argued that it proved that Jinnah's priority had never been Pakistan and that his aim of having Hindus and Muslims looked upon as equals within a united India had failed.[406] Stanley Wolpert, Jinnah's biographer, looks upon the address with disbelief. "What was he talking about? Had he simply forgotten where he was? Had the 'cyclone of events' so disoriented him that he was arguing the opposition's brief? Was he pleading for a united India – on the eve of Pakistan – before those hundreds of thousands of terrified innocents were slaughtered, fleeing their homes, their fields, their ancestral villages and running to an eternity of oblivion or a refugee camp in a strange land".[407]

---

405. Jinnah's address at the Constituent Assembly August 11, in H.D. Sharma op. cit., p. 408.
406. See Ayesha Jalal, op. cit.
407. Stanley Wolpert: Jinnah of Pakistan, Oxford University Press 1984, p. 340.

And still the killings continued unabated. On 12th August, around 40 people were killed in Lahore of which 34 were non-Muslims. In Amritsar city the police had killed two Muslims and one Hindu, while three Muslims and five Hindus had suffered injuries. According to the information received from General Rees, Sikhs had killed 200 Muslims in a village near Jandiala and the Boundary Force had in an encounter with a Sikh gang killed 61 of them. In Gurdaspur, the police had shot one Muslim and one Hindu and four Muslims had died in a communal clash. In Sialkot two Sikhs and one Muslim were stabbed. One Muslim was killed during a raid against a village in Ludhiana district. In another incident, a bomb killed two Muslims and wounded eight in Ferozepore besides killing two non-Muslims.[408]

In a final telegram on 14th August, Jenkins further elaborated on a situation that could be best described as being out of control. In retaliation to the Sikh activities in the central Punjab, Muslims in the Rawalpindi area had attacked two trains. However, the Governor stated that the situation now would be for the new Governments to deal with.[409] A statement, which clearly emphasises that, the British at this point were more concerned with their own safety and exit than securing a peaceful transfer of power. For the British, however, leaving India was also a very

---

408. Governor's letter to the Viceroy dated 13th August 1947, IOL, L/P&J/5/250, p. 6.
409. Jenkins to Mountbatten, telegram 14th August 1947, TOP vol. 12, p. 732.

emotional affair. In his last letter to the Viceroy, the Governor made this final remark: "This is, I suppose, the last letter to be sent by a British Governor of the Punjab to a British Viceroy. It takes with it my very best wishes to your Excellency".[410]

Summary

The internecine strife between Muslims and Sikhs/Hindus continued unhindered from June till 15th August. The cities of Lahore and Amritsar especially surrendered to violence and chaos as small but well organised groups conducted arson, bombing and stabbing. Towards the end even the trains and columns of refugees were attacked.

The Partition Plan from 3rd June was, as expected, met with reluctance hence the major disagreement between the communities remained. There was no agreement as to where the boundary line should be drawn. The Sikhs suddenly started realising that their community would be the biggest loser in the partition. Being both the smallest and the most scattered community of Punjab, the Sikhs

---

410. Governor's letter to the Viceroy dated 13th July 1947, IOL, L/P&J/5/250, p. 4. As with all the letters sent between the Governor and the Viceroy, a minute on the letters content was attached. On the backside of this attachment, dated 30th September 1947, the following comment on the situation in the province was written (in hand) by E. W.R. Lumby: "This is an ancient story already. But it is worth reading because it shows how Sir E. Jenkins appreciated the situation at the crucial moment. Two points of special interest (a) the Governor's alarm, which has proved so amply justified, at the small size of the Boundary Force and (b) his apparent unawareness of any organised Sikh plan, such as is so frequently said to have existed". Ibid.

were mainly located in the central parts. But their numbers were too few and their inhabitation too diverse to avoid being divided in two almost equally large groups in a partition conducted mainly on religious affiliation. The primary fear of the Sikhs was to be caught 'unprepared' as they had been in March during the Rawalpindi massacre. The Muslims had failed to understand how badly the Rawalpindi killings had terrified the Sikh community. Not only were they arming themselves, they had also begun revenging the Rawalpindi massacre. The unprecedented bloodshed was not unexpected as the membership of the private armies was in the neighbourhood of 110,000 by August 1st.

The death toll from 1947 exceeded 3300 by mid May and in many of the fortnightly reports Punjab was referred to as a province in a virtual state of (civil) war. All the three communities trusted neither the British nor the All India political leadership. Therefore, a promise to protect minorities and the establishment of the Punjab Boundary Force could not halt the exodus. The violence in the province became more organised during the period with attacks being directed against mixed villages. The police force was declared indisciplined and unreliable by August and there was even evidence of police officers participating in looting, arson and killing. The community leaders were also accused of having taken part in the disturbances, either directly or by aiding the perpetrators. The Sikh leader, Master Tara Singh, was even recommended for arrest and it was the Governor's opinion that the party organisations were supplying the perpetrators with money and arms and thereby consenting to the violence. It was a combination of 'looking the other way', a British trademark, and aiding and abetting by the communal leaders that made people increasingly aware of genocidal violence as a political option.

As the Independence Day on 15th August came closer it became apparent that partition 'undoubtedly' would be followed by disorder. To avoid British responsibility in the expected mass violence the Viceroy decided to postpone the announcement of the Boundary Commission Award until after transfer of power. The irony was that while Pakistanis and Indians on 15th August awoke to freedom, those living in the disputed areas of central Punjab, in their first moments of freedom, did not know whether they belonged to India or Pakistan.

PART III

INDEPENDENCE

Chapter 6
Ethnic Cleansing and Genocide

August – December 1947

On 15th August 1947 Jawaharlal Nehru, the first Prime Minister addressed the independent India from the Central Hall of Parliament and "redeemed his tryst with destiny". Even though indirectly referring to the events in Punjab and Bengal, Nehru's address was, understandably, a speech for the future. "Before the birth of freedom we have endured all the pains of labour and our hearts are heavy with the memory of the sorrow. Some of those pains continue even now. Nevertheless the past is over and it is the future that beckons to us now".[411] Interestingly the 'father of the nation' decided not to take part in the independence celebrations. Disillusioned by the partition, the massive violence and for being sidelined by the Congress leadership, Mahatma Gandhi stayed out of Delhi.[412] Instead he went to Calcutta to appeal to Hindus and Muslims to live in peace. However, nobody went to Punjab where millions were on the move as refugees while thousands were already killed, abducted or raped. The newly partitioned province had completely surrendered to violence and chaos.

---

411. Nehru's address at the Constituent Assembly August 14, in H.D. Sharma, op. cit., p. 417.
412. Stanley Wolpert: Gandhi's Passion. The Life and Legacy of Mahatma Gandhi, Oxford University Press 2001, p. 10.

The announcement of the Boundary Award on 16th August fuelled the communal frenzy as each community felt that it was being denied the right to its homeland. While Pakistan was granted an area of 63.000 square miles of the Punjab province, only 37.000 square miles remained on the Indian side. Though the main guideline for the Commission was to draw a borderline along religious affiliations, the diversity of the Punjabi population rendered the task almost impossible. Instead of creating religious majority states, all it managed to do was to create isolated islands of religious minorities. At the time of the partition, roughly 1/3 of the Punjabi population lived on the wrong side of the border. In eastern Punjab the minority numbered around 35 % minority and in western Punjab the number was 25 %.[413]

Therefore, the mass violence and exodus was rendered inevitable. The newly appointed Governor of West Punjab (in Pakistan), Sir Francis Mudie, described the general situation, as "festered with tension". A day before the actual partition a Gurudwara (Sikh temple) was destroyed in Lahore and between 13 and 22 Sikhs were killed. The news from outside Lahore was scarce, but the Governor mentioned one incident from the Gurdaspur-Sialkot border where Muslims had attacked a train and killed about 100 Hindus and Sikhs.[414] Even though efforts were made by leaders of

---

413. Tan Tai Young (1997), op., cit., pp. 14-15.
414. Mudie to Jinnah, 15th August 1947, in Kirpal Singh: "The Partition of Punjab 1947", Delhi 199, pp. 488-489.

both Sikhs and Muslims to persuade their followers to stop the attacks, it was increasingly becoming difficult since most outrages were committed in retaliation.

Field Marshall Sir Claude Auchinleck, the Supreme Commander in India and Pakistan held Sikhs responsible for the violence in Amritsar and the surrounding areas. At a meeting of the Joint Defence Council he argued that Sikhs "were operating in armed bands of considerable strength and carrying out raids against Muslim villages, or the Muslim parts of larger villages - three or four raids nightly. These bands were well organised and often included mounted men for reconnaissance purposes. One band was reported to have killed 200 Muslims in one village".[415] It was suspected that even the Sikh princely states like Patiala and Faridkot were involved in assisting these raids. The bands of Muslims were also operating but they were usually smaller and less organised. According to the Supreme Commander the number of civilian casualties, in the area where the Boundary force operated, was estimated at 1.500 killed and wounded, in addition to over 200 killed and wounded by the troops.[416]

He emphasised that both Lahore and Amritsar police forces were considered completely unreliable. In Lahore the

---

415. Minutes of the Joint Defence Council Meeting, 16th August 1947, in Kirpal Singh: "The Partition of Punjab 1947", Delhi 1991, pp. 489-494. At the Council meeting were Lord Mountbatten, Sarder Baldev Singh, The Pakistani High Commissioner, Field Marshall Auchinleck
416. Ibid.

police force had actually joined the mobs in arson and killing of non-Muslims. The Boundary Force was therefore the only body left to enforce law and order. Auchinleck praised it for behaving impartially and for having successfully encountered with bands from all the three communities and mentioned an occasion where 60 perpetrators had been killed. However, he found it impossible to protect every village or hamlet, unless troops were "permanently posted". In Lahore, the Supreme Commander opined that the Muslim League National Guards were involved in the attacks and that they had encouraged the Muslim mobs. By 16th August around 10-15% of Lahore appeared to have been burned down and the vicinities were also considerably affected. The Railways were badly hit too, and all traffic on the Amritsar - Lahore line had been suspended. The trouble had now spread to Sialkot and Gujranwala where a train had been held up and 100 persons killed and 200 wounded.

At the Joint Defence Council meeting Nehru raised his concern as to why the trains were being attacked despite being provided with a military escort. Auchinleck described the *modus operandi* of the gangs as either entering the train on a station and then attacking suddenly, "or put one man on the train to pull the communication cord at the spot where the rest of the gang was ready".[417] The perpetrators often had information about train schedules, which pointed

---

417. Ibid.

towards a high degree of organisation and some complicity by railway officials.[418] At the meeting the responsibility for the disturbances were also debated. Even though the Sikh representative, Sardar Baldev Singh, did not openly discharge the accusations against his community, he did point out that the trouble in the Punjab had started in Rawalpindi, where Sikhs had been massacred by Muslims. Massacres that the Muslim League had never condemned.[419] On the more positive side, however, Auchinleck mentioned that efforts were made to arrange a meeting between the Sikh leaders from Amritsar and the Muslim League leaders from Lahore. The conclusion of the Joint Defence Council meeting, it was decided not to impose martial law at the moment.

On 20th August the situation improved slightly in Lahore, Amritsar, Sialkot and Gujranwala, while it deteriorated in the rural areas of Jullundur, Hoshiarpur and Gurdaspur. An unprecedented mass exodus started around this time. At the end of August there were hardly any non-Muslims left in Lahore, compared to the 300.000 prior to the rioting.[420] The Mayor of Lahore at the time of partition, Mian Amiruddin, narrates the war-like situation in Lahore in this way "The Shahalmi area within the walled city of Lahore was the stronghold of the Hindus. It was like an

418. Swarna Aiyar (1998), op., cit., p. 23.
419. Minutes of the Joint Defence Council Meeting, 16th August 1947, in Kirpal Singh: "The Partition of Punjab 1947", Delhi 1991, pp. 489-494.
420. G. D. Khosla, op., cit., p. 125.

impregnable fortress. Countless weapons and ammunition were stored there, and the Hindus were sure that nothing could happen to Shahalmi. But when we launched our (Molotov) cocktails the Shahalmi fort could not withstand the attack. As the locality burned down, the Hindus lost heart and began to move towards Amritsar".[421]

The central districts i.e. those touched by the boundary line had by now surrendered to chaos. The refugee camps were in a very poor state and the lack of proper sanitary arrangements increased the danger of a cholera outbreak. The camps, no more than 5-6 accommodated well over 100.000 people and were in desperate need of tents and medical facilities[422].

In Sheikhupura, on 26th August, a band of Baluch (Pakistani) soldiers organised a huge massacre on non-Muslims. Around ten thousands were killed and many girls molested. The attacks were now becoming frequent. The abduction, molestation or rape of women was a weapon to humiliate the men as being unable to protect the community honour. The use of rape in military campaigns to demoralise the enemy is not a new feature.[423] However, in Punjab many women were either killed by their kinsmen or committed

---

421. Mian Amiruddin. "Memories of Partition", in Ahmad Salim (ed.), op. cit., p. 255.
422. Minute of the Joint Defence Council Meeting, 20th August 1947, in Kirpal Singh: "The Partition of Punjab 1947", Delhi 1991, pp. 495-496.
423. Ruth Harris: "The 'Child of the Barbarian'; Rape, Race and Nationalism in France during the First World War", in Past and Present, 141, (Nov. 1993) p. 170-206.

suicide to save their honour. Urvashi Butalia in her landmark work on the oral histories of the women in Partition, *The Other Side of Silence,* gives voice to a man who narrates how his father killed his sister:

"When my father swung the kirpan (sword) perhaps some doubt or fear came into his mind, or perhaps the kirpan got stuck in her dupatta (head scarf), no one can say. It was such a frightening, such a fearful scene. Then my sister, with her own hand removed her plait and pulled it forward...and my father with his own hands moved her dupatta aside and then he swung the kirpan and her head and neck rolled off and fell...there...far away."[424]

This story testifies to the ultimate sacrifice for the religion where, interestingly, the father is described as much as a victim as his daughter. According to an eyewitness account several non-Muslims killed their "young girls to save their honour" at the above-mentioned Sheikhupura massacre. The witness also narrated how a baby-boy was snatched from his mother and then cut into two. The mother was afterwards stabbed with a spear.[425] The targeting of female members of a community occurred in other districts too. At a village in Sialkot district relatives of a girl were

424. Urvashi Butalia (1998), op., cit., p. 171.
425. G.D. Khosla, op., cit, p. 156.

forced to stand around while she was continuously raped.[426] In Montgomery district caravans of refugees, on their way to the Indian Dominion, were attacked and men and women butchered and young girls abducted.[427] During an attack on a village in Shahpur district by end August, survivors were forcibly converted to Islam and forced to eat beef. At other places men were circumcised on the spot.[428]

The recurring feature in these attacks was the emphasis on the symbols of sexuality and reproduction as the female body presented an opportunity to conquer the enemy territory. The attacks on the women were made on two levels: firstly, women as an embodiment of the community honour and secondly, their bodies as the site of community reproduction. The modus operandi included gang rapes, stripping, parading naked women through the town, branding the breasts and genitalia with slogans like 'Pakistan Zindabad[429]' or 'Hindustan Zindabad', amputating the breasts, knifing open the womb and killing the foetuses. The rape especially was used as a weapon not just to humiliate the 'other', but also to sow one's own seed in the enemy womb. Thus each community acknowledged the role of women as the bearers of future generation. Those women who were impregnated with the 'bad seed' were at times forced to undergo abortion to maintain the purity of the

426. Ibid., p. 146.
427. Ibid., p. 161.
428. Ibid., p. 173.
429. Zindabad means Long Live.

162

community.[430] It has, however, been pointed out that women were not only victims but also sometimes provided "moral support or backing for at least a proportion of the violence that occurred".[431]

The sexual violence was not limited to women alone but also brought men in its orbit. The men were either castrated or forcibly circumcised in many cases. Sudhir Kakkar suggests that "cutting off breasts or the male castration incorporates the more or less conscious wish to wipe the hated enemy off the face of earth by eliminating the means of its reproduction and the nurturing of its infants".[432] Likewise the attack on children was based on a similar premise and the perpetrators showed no mercy to a generation which could become belligerent in future. These specific features are a pointer to the genocidal intent in the partition violence. Other weapon used in the conflict was the abuse of religious symbols sacred to the other community. It included forcible religious conversion, forcing Hindus to eat beef or Muslims to eat pork, burning scriptures or places of worship. For example in Montgomery district it was reported that those non-Muslim incapable of leaving were forced to convert to Islam. Their holy books, the Guru Granth Sahib (holy Sikh script) and various sacred Hindu

430. Urvashi Butalia, (1998), op., cit.
431. Sarah Ansari: "Pakistan, Partition and Gender: Fashioning the Shape of Pakistani Womanhood", in International Journal of Punjab Studies, vol. 6, no. 1, 1999, p. 19.
432. Sudhir Kakkar, op. cit. p 37.

scriptures were burnt and places of worship like the Gurudwaras and temples were destroyed.[433] These kinds of attacks were of course not limited to the non-Muslim population. A significant number of Mosques were also destroyed and many Muslim women abducted and raped.

Due to non accessibility to the official Pakistani account of the violence, this study has mainly relied on the reports and accounts by various officials, including British, Indian and Pakistani, who were directly involved in the Partition process. Several secondary literatures suggest that the violence committed against the Muslims matched the violence endured by the non-Muslims. In this context, it is important to emphasise that the aim of this study is not to place a historical judgement on any of the three communities, but to illustrate and explain the manifestation of the violence. The most important characteristic of Punjab in August 1947 was that the entire province was engulfed by the violence. It was *de facto* engaged in a civil war.

The great outburst of communal frenzy also affected the Boundary Force. On 26th August, only a week after having praised the very same troops for their impartiality, Auchinleck stated, "he would be unable to guarantee the reliability and general impartiality of the troops under his command beyond the middle of September".[434] The position

---

433. Report of work in the Montgomery district, Kirpal Singh, op., cit., p. 642.
434. Note for the Joint Defence Council by the Supreme Commander on the future of the Punjab Boundary Force, 26th August 1947, in Kirpal Singh op., cit., pp. 500-502.

of the Boundary Force was described as "impossible".[435] The disturbances had now spread to parts of Punjab outside its realm of operation as 70 % of attacks on trains happened outside its area. Another concern was that the Force had had to handle affairs it wasn't meant to deal with, such as political and administrative problems. The Supreme Commander proposed to close down the Force and leave it to the two new states to enforce law and order.

At the same time the magnitude of the refugee problem had gone beyond the control of the Governments of India and Pakistan and, according to Auchinleck, it appeared as if civil Government had ceased to exist in eastern Punjab. He recommended that each state should put up new military headquarters on each side on the border with Liaison officers attached. The process of separating the soldiers into two armies should be under close supervision to avoid clashes between them, and it was suggested that a neutral zone should be established between the forward posts of the two new armies to reduce the risk of them fighting each other.

The Indian High Commissioner[436] situated in Lahore, on 27th August, criticised both the Boundary force and the Government for western Punjab for doing nothing to counter the attacks on Hindus and Sikhs. The Pakistani officials

---

435. Ibid.
436. Immediately after independence both states established diplomatic representations ("High Commissioners") with each other.

were allegedly only concerned with the situation in eastern Punjab and the High Commissioner opined that a wholesale slaughter of Sikhs could be expected if conditions did not improve in eastern Punjab immediately. He estimated that 40.000 lives would be in danger during the next 48 hours and therefore recommended a transfer of population.[437]

Amidst massive critique. a Joint Defence Council meeting on 29th August decided to abolish the Punjab Boundary Force from midnight 31st August/1st September.[438] After the failure of the Boundary force, the task of maintaining law and order in Punjab was taken over by India and Pakistan. To show their determination, the Prime Minister of Pakistan Liaqat Ali Khan and the Prime Minister of India Jawaharlal Nehru released a joint statement on 3rd September calling on all communities to end the atrocities. They assured that all powers of the Governments would be used against the perpetrators. "Bands caught in the act of committing crime will be shot at sight".[439] However, the totality of the distrust among the Punjabi peoples was manifested by the Prime Ministers assurances that refugee camps would be guarded by military in which the refugees

437. High Commissioner for India to Nehru, 27th August 1947, in Kirpal Singh op., cit., pp. 502-503.
438. Minute of the sixth meeting of the Joint Defence Council, 29th August 1947, in Kirpal Singh, op., cit., pp. 503-508. Present at the meeting. Mounbatten, Jinnah, Nehru, Liaquat Ali Khan, Baldev Singh, Mudie, Trivedi, Auchinleck and Rees.
439. Joint Statement of Nehru and Ali Khan, in Kirpal Singh op., cit., pp. 508-509.

had confidence, i.e. members of their own community.[440] Governor Mudie, though, was doubtful whether it would be feasible to protect refugee camps and convoys with soldiers of their own nationality, since he found it crucial to try "and keep the two armies apart".[441]

In the beginning of September the ethnic cleansing had reached gigantic proportions. According to Mudie, the number of refugees crossing the border daily was between 100.000 and 150.000. He blamed the Sikhs particularly for this mass migration. In his view it was essential to get the Sikhs out of the province. "I am telling every one that I don't care how the Sikhs get across the border; the great thing is to get rid of them as soon as possible".[442]

The Governor for eastern Punjab, Sir Trivedi also blamed the Sikhs. In his view they were responsible for obstructing the peace in the eastern part[443] and he was convinced that their activities were organised even though Sikh leaders like Tara Singh and Giani Kartar Singh were doing all they could to restore peace. Their appeals, however, neither reached the interior of eastern Punjab nor the low-level leaders. By mid- September, the raids conducted by armed bands of Sikhs affected practically every

440. Gopi Chand Bhargava to Nehru, 4th September 1947, in Kirpal Singh, op., cit., pp. 509-510.
441. Mudie to Jinnah, 5th September 1947, in Kirpal Singh, op., cit., pp. 511-513.
442. Ibid.
443. Trivedi to Swaran Singh, 4th September 1947, in Kirpal Singh, op., cit., pp. 510-511.

district of Jullundur division. One such band had attacked a refugee caravan near Dera Baba Nanak Railway Station and in Jullundur a refugee train had been derailed. A convoy of Muslim refugees proceeding from north to south was also attacked by large bands of Sikhs armed with rifles and the number of casualties was reportedly very heavy. In an almost desperate tone Trivedi stressed upon the importance of peaceful evacuations in order to protect the large number of non-Muslims still waiting to be evacuated from western Punjab. According to Trivedi it had been emphasised by Governor Mudie that the organised massacres by Sikhs on Muslims "naturally" were producing "a violent reaction" in western Punjab.[444] In many cases, the refugees after having reached their safe haven caused an increase in tension while they narrated their stories. There were even examples of refugee columns attacking each other while passing.[445]

The incidents of retaliation were especially prominent in cases of train attacks. Whenever a 'ghost train' laden with dead bodies arrived on one side, another would immediately be sent in the opposite direction.[446] According to a British officer the "murder, brutality, looting, ill treatment of women and small children in evacuee trains" had exceeded even "Belsen and other bestialities created by the warped Nazi mind".[447]

---

444. Trivedi to Swaran Singh, 12th September 1947, in Kirpal Singh, op., cit., pp. 523-524.
445. Swarna Aiyar (1994), op., cit., p. 131. Many of the large columns were several miles long.
446. Tucker, While memory serves, p. 480.
447. Ibid., p. 482.

The inhuman situation for refugees in eastern Punjab caused great concern among the Muslim leaders. An immediate evacuation of every single Muslim still alive was demanded and the east Punjab authorities were accused of not honouring international decisions.[448] Mudie forwarded the accusation in a letter to Trivedi where he expressed his worries about the "complete breakdown of law and order" along with the Government's "surrender" to the Sikhs, whom he again particularly blamed for the carnage. According to Mudie's information, Sikhs were controlling the passage through Amritsar which had serious consequences for the refugees. Even though he acknowledged that "very regrettable things had happened in west Punjab", he nevertheless emphasised that these were isolated incidents compared to east Punjab where Sikhs were executing a well organised plan to exterminate Muslims or drive them out of the Province.[449] He further argued that while Sikhs had been driven out in many cases, their exodus from central districts like Montgomery and Lyallpur had been voluntary and well planned and even intended by Sikh leaders like Giani Kartar Singh, though the districts were still undisturbed: "Therein - in the matter of organisation - lies the difference between the East and West Punjab",[450] was his conclusion.

---

448. Premier of west Punjab to Prime Minister Pakistan, 12th September 1947, in Kirpal Singh, op., cit., p. 524.
449. Mudie to Trivedi, 17th September 1947, in Kirpal Singh, op., cit., pp. 525-526.
450. Ibid.

The partition proved disastrous especially for the Sikhs and can therefore be linked to the unprecedented scale of violence. As the smallest of the Punjabi communities they risked being divided into two groups and their earlier threats of violence were now effectuated. Nevertheless, the serious critique of the Sikh community for committing atrocities was discharged on 17th September by the Home Minister for eastern Punjab, Swaran Singh (a Sikh himself). In his view only sporadic and local outburst of violence had occurred and there was no evidence of an organised effort. He further emphasised that armed bands and lawlessness were not confined to one community only and were breeding in an atmosphere of anger, uncertainty and revenge. He felt that the longing for revenge was an important motivator. "We cannot however ignore the feelings of anger and excitement in which our refugees from the West Punjab find themselves. Their woeful tales of suffering create an atmosphere, in which sentiments of retaliation has the upper hand".[451] Singh's defence of the Sikhs clearly manifests as to how difficult, if not impossible, it was to delink oneself from the fate of one's community.

But it was not the local officials alone who were affected by such emotions. Governor Mudie wrote on 23rd September in a letter to Jinnah that. "We have told the Sikh Major-

---

451. Swaran Singh to Trivedi, 17th September 1947, in Kirpal Singh, op., cit., pp. 526-528.

General who, is in command at Amritsar that unless our people are allowed through Amritsar we will hold the Sikhs who left Lyallpur about a week ago and who are now about to cross the Sutlej to East Punjab. This is said to have made a considerable impression on him".[452] The Governor maintained that not only had the east Punjab Government lost control, but the Sikhs were still carrying out atrocities and now even Muslims in Delhi were being attacked. In his view it would be impossible for Muslims to remain in eastern Punjab and all of the 5,4 million Muslims would have to be accommodated in the west. He then asked rhetorically. "How can we accommodate these people unless we get rid of the Hindus and Sikhs. All or practically all Hindus and Sikhs would have to leave western Punjab, if not for any other reason than to make room for the Muslims who had been forced out of eastern Punjab".[453] This statement showed a whole new rationale in the ethnic cleansing. A rationale that was legitimised by making the protection of ones own community as the priority.

The intent of altering the demographic outlook was also effectively proved with the way the enemy property was attacked. This time the property, especially houses, weren't destroyed in the same way as during the March riots. Those who were forced out were not expected to

---

452. Mudie to Jinnah, 23rd September 1947, in Kirpal Singh, op., cit., pp. 529-531.
453. Ibid.

171

return; instead their property was left so that the new comers could move in.[454]

Colonel Sher Khan (from Pakistan) presented, in a report to Governor Mudie on 24th September, a rather gloomy picture of the situation in eastern Punjab. He had arrived in eastern Punjab on 16th and found that the civil administration was totally ineffective. From 16th to 21st September the number of attacks on Muslims had been less frequent, but this was largely due to the fact that "there were no Muslims left to be attacked".[455] Nevertheless, from 21st September, the attacks on trains and refugee columns had resumed in Amritsar and Jullundur districts. The train raids on 21st night and 22nd night had been particularly vicious leaving the refugees killed, wounded or abducted and the trains subsequently looted. The Colonel on 22nd night even witnessed the police participation in attacking and looting. The non-Muslim troops also proved incapable of protecting the refugees. In some cases it was even alleged that they had joined the attackers, but the Colonel could not verify the claim. Nonetheless, he was convinced that the troops had knowledge of when large-scale attacks were about to take place and conveniently deployed themselves, only to re-emerge after "the damage was done".

---

454. Swarna Aiyar (1994), op., cit., 114.
455. Col. Sherkhan's Report of East Punjab, 24th September 1947, in Kirpal Singh, op., cit., pp. 536-538.

172

In his view the attacks were part of a twin political objective of the Akalis and the RSS to throw Muslims out of Punjab and even India and in the process discrediting the Congress and other "democratic bodies and establish fascism". The unintended consequences of this aim, however, was also hurting non-Muslims and especially Sikhs in western Punjab who expressed bitterness towards the Akalis and begged them to end the killings of Muslims, since Sikhs subsequently would be killed in retaliation. This circle of attacks, counter-attacks, revenge and retaliation made it extremely difficult to evacuate refugees from both East and West Punjab.

In his reply to Home Minister Swaran Singh, Governor Trivedi on 26th September described a similar development. Up till 20th September (since the 12th) the general situation had begun to improve. From 21st and onwards, however, things had deteriorated badly. Governor Trivedi disagreed with Singh concerning whether the lawless activities were unorganised. "There is undoubtedly an organisation behind attacks on refugee trains. Hundreds of people cannot collect together without some kind of previous arrangement".[456]

The level of organisation and the military conduct in the attacks is not particularly surprising given the military

---

456. Trivedi to Swaran Singh, 26th September 1947, in Kirpal Singh, op., cit., pp. 538-541.

173

tradition of Punjab into account. During the colonial rule Punjabi men formed the backbone of the British Indian Army. At the outbreak of the Second World War Punjabi men constituted roughly 48% of manpower in the British Indian Army. For Punjab it meant that one out of every three men at the age between 17 and 30 had served in the army during the war.[457] Following their demobilisation in 1945 many ex-soldiers had joined the various private armies in the province. Governor Trivedi further criticised Singh indirectly for not being impartial and effective enough in taking disciplinary actions against those officials who had indulged in looting, besides showing unwillingness to take unpopular measures to enforce law and order. As an example the Governor mentioned his proposal of banning Kirpans (swords) in public, which Swaran Singh opposed strongly in a cabinet meeting on 24th. Even though he recognised that each Muslim killed in eastern Punjab was an invitation for retaliation on the other side of the border, he discharged Singh's point of view that feelings of anger and revenge could not be ignored, by arguing that "these feelings cannot and ought not determine our policy".[458].

A British Police officer wrote on 23rd September that the situation in both parts of Punjab had improved and there was no "killing, looting or burning of villages" This, however,

---

457. Swarna Aiyar (1998), op., cit., pp. 24-25.
458. Ibid.

was because all Sikhs and Hindus in western Punjab and all Muslims from eastern Punjab had now left for camps. "The only incidents that occur now are attacks on convoys, caravans and evacuee trains".[459] According to him these attacks were becoming less frequent due to better protection. However, at the end of September the number of killed, on each side, was estimated between 100.000 and 200.000 by one of the commanding officers General Tucker.[460]

The vulnerability of Hindus and Sikhs in western Punjab where they were in minority had resulted in massacres and ethnic cleansing. Thus, in the Shahpur district many Hindus and Sikhs had been forcefully converted and in Gujrat and Dera Ghazi Khan districts non-Muslims had suffered "heavy casualties" amidst all sorts of atrocities. In Jhelum, on 26th September, a larger number of non-Muslims including women and children were slaughtered. Lahore was still badly affected and hardly a day went by without violent incidents taking place.[461] The lives of non-Muslims in western Punjab were unsafe and even their evacuation could turn out to be difficult unless measures "to control the situation" were taken.[462]

459. Tucker, op., cit., p. 489.
460. Ibid., p. 491.
461. Chief Liaison Officer east Punjab Government to Chief Secretary west Punjab Government, 4th October 1947, in Kirpal Singh op., cit.; pp. 542-543.
462. Ibid.

During the September carnage too, the women and children were targeted especially. At Harnoil in the Mianwali district fierce fighting took place around the third week between the Hindu population and Muslim mobs. The attack was organised with the help of Muslim military that also used tanks. More than half of the 6000 inhabitants were massacred and "children were snatched away from their mothers arms and thrown into the boiling oil. Hundreds of women saved their honour by jumping into wells or throwing themselves into burning houses, thus burnt themselves alive. Girls of 8 to 10 years of age were raped in the presence of their parents and then put to death mercilessly. There were stories of women having their breast cut off and they were made to walk all naked in rows of five in the bazaars of Harnoil. About 800 girls and women were abducted and small kiddies were wandering without a cover in the jungles and were kidnapped by the passers-by".[463] It was almost a repetition of the earlier massacres characterised by the unprecedented atrocities committed against women and children.

Richard Symonds, who at that time worked as relief worker in western Punjab, narrates an incident from October 16, where he along with Lady Mountbatten in Lahore, met Governor Mudie. During the meeting, the Governor, who earlier had expressed the need to get rid of Sikhs and Hindus,

---

463. Report of work of Liaison Agency in District Mianwali, in Kirpal Singh op., cit., p. 677.

stated (not surprisingly) that he favoured a complete evacuation of non-Muslims. He furthermore emphasised that he "hoped that the Pakistan Government Minister, Ghazanfar Ali, would fail in his current attempts to persuade them to remain".[464] In this situation the Governments of India and Pakistan decided to prepare a 'Joint Evacuation Movement Plan' on 20th October. According to the 1941 census there were 5,3 million Muslims in eastern Punjab and 3,8 million non-Muslims in western Punjab.[465] It was estimated that since 1st August 1947 2,1 million Muslims had left eastern Punjab and 2 million non-Muslims western Punjab.

Joint Evacuation Movement Plan[466]

	MUSLIMS	NON-MUSLIMS
At present	3.2 million	1.8 million
On completion of Non-Muslim foot convoy (approx. 1 Nov.)	2.4 million	1.2 million
On completion of Muslim foot convoy (estimate on 30 Nov.)	500.000	600.000
On 15 Dec.	250.000	300.000
On 31 Dec.	NIL	NIL

According to the Joint Evacuation Movement Plan, the remaining 3,2 million Muslims in eastern Punjab and 1,8

464. Richard Symonds, op., cit., p. 49.
465. Joint Evacuation Movement Plan, 20th October 1947, in Kirpal Singh, op., cit., pp. 548-552. The number of Hindus were 2.3 million and Sikhs made up 1.5 millions.
466. Ibid.

million non-Muslims in western Punjab were to be moved across the border, either in foot convoys, motor transport convoys or by trains. The whole transfer of population was supposed to be completed at the end of December so that no Muslims would remain in eastern Punjab and no non-Muslims in western Punjab.

The Plan also envisaged that 100.000 people would leave on foot every 3 days on different routes and it was estimated that it would take 12 days to move the non-Muslims and 35 days for the Muslims. By rail 15.000 were to be moved in each direction daily, for a period of 70 days. The motor transport convoy was estimated to lift 800 Muslims daily and 4.500 non-Muslims for a total period of 46 days. A great problem was the shortage of troops for protection of the marching columns along with the risk of delays. Even if everything went according to plan, it would still take till the end of the year before all refugees were evacuated.

Secondly, the two Governments also agreed that, "conversions by people abducted after 1st March 47 will not be recognized and all such persons must be restored to their respective Dominions. The wishes of the persons concerned are irrelevant".[467] In the agreement it was emphasised that the recovering and removing of women should be undertaken

---

467. Agreement of India and Pakistan Governments for Recovery of Abducted women, 6th December 1947, in Kirpal Singh op., cit., pp. 572-573.

disregarding the wish of the women themselves. Furthermore "any children which they may have produced in the interim were to be left behind, with retrospective effect from 1 March 1947".[468] On 16th December 1947 Mudie wrote to Jinnah that, "our exchange of population is practically over now".[469]

Thirdly, and most importantly, the task before the JEM plan was to recover the ten of thousands of abducted women and children. The process of the recovery was both long and difficult. The authorities on either side did not always follow the agreement for recovery and some of the women found it difficult to leave the new surroundings where they had rooted themselves. This was especially the case for those who had given birth during their years in abduction. They were faced with a dilemma, whether to leave their children or not. Around ten years after the partition, in 1957, the search for women had almost petered out. At that time a total of 35,863 had been recovered from both India and Pakistan out of an estimated number of 45,000.[470]

Though the violence subsided slowly after reaching a peak in August - September, it left indelible scars in the minds and lives of the survivors. They did not even have the luxury to mourn their fate or that of their dead ones, as the immediate task was to get on with the business of reconstruction.

---

468. Sarah Ansari, op., cit., p. 21.
469. Mudie to Jinnah, 16th December 1947, in Kirpal Singh op., cit., pp. 575-576.
470. Andrew J. Major: "The Chief Sufferers': Abduction of women During the Partition of the Punjab", in D. A. Low (ed.) (1998), op., cit., p. 65.

Summary

Along with the independence and the inevitable partition in August 1947, a carnage swept through Punjab that exceeded even the worst imaginable fears. The magnitude and brutality of the violence was unprecedented. The trains and all other means of railroad transport were attacked with military precision. Village after village was levelled to the ground where men, women and children were massacred en masse in a spiral of attacks, counter-attacks, retaliation and revenge. The total breakdown of the cultural order was manifested with the brutal attacks on women. Many men killed female relatives to 'save their honour'.

The mass violence also triggered off a massive migration. More than nine million people or around one third of Punjabis crossed the border between August and December 1947. This exodus did not happen voluntarily but was forced upon Muslims, Hindus and Sikhs as they were being consistently attacked. The people were forced to leave their home and hearth because of their fear of becoming a minority in a given place. The religious affiliations were the sole criterion that decided where people could live. It was undisputedly a case of ethnic cleansing.

This ethnic cleansing was further accompanied by genocidal massacres where whole or parts of villages were destroyed. The violence was neither unorganised nor spontaneous. The train attacks, distribution of weapons and attacks by outsiders on the villages testified to an organised effort. The private armies committed most of the atrocities but were also aided by ordinary people. The law and order institutions were incapable of protecting people and in many cases actually acted as perpetrators. After the Punjab Boundary Force's surrender to the 'communal virus' and abolition from 1st September, the last illusion of the protection of people vanished. At the end of October, a mass exchange of population was organised which was completed by mid December. This also brought the large-scale ethnic cleansing to a culmination, though the genocidal massacres petered out only because there was nobody left to kill.

Conclusions

In this book, I have attempted to describe the development of the communal violence in Punjab 1937- 47, and to identify the violence that occurred in last part of this period as genocidal. The violence that immediately preceded partition was sharply distinct from the communal violence that has prevailed in colonial and post-colonial India (one exception perhaps being the 1984 anti-Sikh violence in Delhi).

The political power struggle played a huge role in altering the manifestation of violence. The relationship between the three communities was shaped largely by the impetus given by the national political events. The introduction of political autonomy, following the Government of India Act, 1935, triggered off a struggle for political supremacy in Punjab. The key player in the Punjab politics, the Unionist Party, which emerged victorious in the 1937 provincial elections was faced with the political challenge posed by Mohammad Ali Jinnah. The Sikandar-Jinnah pact from October 1937 provided Jinnah with the right to negotiate on behalf of the Punjabi Muslims at the Centre, on the condition that he stayed out of Punjabi politics. For Sikander Hyat Khan the pact with Jinnah made it possible for him to control the only Muslim opposition to the Unionist Party, as Muslim members of the Unionist Party should assume membership of the League. Having little interest in regional politics, the most important aim for Jinnah was to make the Muslim League a symbol of Muslim Unity.

In 1939, Jinnah's role as the sole representative of the Muslim community was further confirmed by the British decision to negotiate the issue of framing a post-war Constitution with all the communities and not only with the Congress, the main political party.

The entry of Jinnah into Punjab politics by 1940 challenged the multi-religious character of the province. In the Lahore resolution on 23rd March 1940, Jinnah clearly articulated the exclusivity of Muslims as a nation, thus, sharpening the communal cleavages among the three communities. Though it is a matter of debate if Jinnah proposed the resolution as a mere bargaining counter, it did succeed in alarming the minority Sikh community towards a perceived Muslim aggression. The regional politics, which under the Unionists was mainly a struggle for supremacy within the Muslim community, was now suffused with communal propaganda. The Punjabi Muslims were proclaimed as a separate entity with nothing in common with the Hindu or Sikh Punjabis. This led to the creation or strengthening of self-defence mechanisms like armed volunteer bands in the each community.

The British, fully aware of the growing estrangement among the three communities, were hesitant to intervene, afraid that it could hamper the war effort. The Cripps Mission in March 1942, despite its failure, kept the possibility of separate Muslim states alive and was followed by a remarkable increase in membership of the RSS. Thus, the fear of communal outbursts remained intact.

As Jinnah appropriated more power at the centre he further tried to challenge the Unionist leadership in the Punjab. This was partly made possible by the sudden demise of Sir Sikander in December 1942. Unlike Sir Sikander, his successor Khizar Hyat Khan did not have the same power-base within the Unionist Party. Thus, Khizar was soon challenged from both within the party and outside by young rural based Muslim leaders. While not wanting to submit to the otherwise hegemonic Unionist Party, Jinnah provided them with a platform to change the political balance. In May 1944 Premier Khizar was expelled from the Muslim League and the reorganisation of Muslim volunteer bands into Muslim League National Guards further testified to the changing political reality. Thus, the Muslim League succeeded both in sidelining the Unionist Party and emerging as the representative of the Punjabi Muslims. The aggressive behaviour of the League further intensified the communal conflict.

The 1945/46 provincial elections, which were fought purely on communal lines, altered the outlook of Punjabi politics. The hegemony of the Unionist, which had been under a strong pressure since 1944, was broken as the

Muslim League emerged as the single largest party. The election campaign conducted on religious lines brought electoral success to the Muslim League but had adverse impact on the inter-communal relation. The League's cry for "Islam in danger" effectively merged politics with religion. This was reinforced with the threats of excommunication to the Muslims, if they failed to vote for the League. The election campaign, which also included the demand for Pakistan, strongly antagonised the Sikhs and Hindus because of its uncompromising communal character. Ironically, Muslim League, the largest political party, failed to form a Government as the Unionist managed to remain in power with the support of Congress and Akalis. Unable to obtain political power, the Muslim League initiated an anti-government agitation that further intensified the communal conflict.

The announcement of the British withdrawal in February 1947 made it utmost important for the League to gain control in the Punjab, since it was made clear that power, if needed, would be transferred to provincial governments. Thus, the agitation was intensified and in early March the Punjab Government resigned followed by severe communal unrest. The Hindus and Sikhs started rioting in Lahore and Amritsar in protest over the fall of the Government. However, the situation further exploded when the League was unable to form a new Government, and yet again saw the political power disappearing, as the Governor took control of the administration. This led to an intensification of the ongoing violence. It was now Muslims who were organising the rioting. The violence, which also engulfed urban areas of central Punjab, was at its worst in the North Western rural districts of the Rawalpindi Division. Here, the number of dead ran into thousands.

The March rioting deepened the psychological divide between Muslims and non-Muslims and was described by the Governor as an 'internecine-strife'. Soon after Hindus and Sikhs started articulating the need for a partition, which was also suggested by an emergency meeting of the Congress Working Committee on March 8. The consistent failures in reaching political agreement at the Centre during April and May, made the demand for Partition more vocal. Following the political deadlock, the partition plan was announced on June 3, with an expected British departure on August 14/15. The partition plan and the imminent transfer did not calm the communal tension. It rather intensified as no agreement concerning the boundary line was reached.

The Sikhs, especially, felt anguished since they, as the smallest and most scattered of the three communities felt that they would be the biggest losers. Having realised, though a little late that a partition based on religious affiliations would mean being cut into two, the Sikhs began arming themselves. They did not want to be caught 'unprepared' as they had been during the Rawalpindi massacres in March. At the same time the estimated membership of the various private armies was by August 1, expected to be 110,000.

While the British authorities prepared to exit, the new power structures in both the states were yet to take shape. There were many reports of the police force being involved in looting, arson and killing. Furthermore, the British on their departure were less than willing to sacrifice the manpower and weaponry needed to check the communal violence. The unprecedented escalation of violence in 1947 puts a question mark on the motives of the British, as there is a constant reference to a possibility of a 'civil war like situation' in the official correspondence since 1946. There was no comprehensive contingency plan to control the mass violence, which they themselves had anticipated all along. The intelligence reports on the activities of the communal leaders, especially Sikhs, clearly pointed towards the expectation of mass violence.

The embryonic states of India and Pakistan were actually ill equipped to control the communal frenzy as the communal divide had deeply affected the officials in the troubled province. In an attempt to calm down people and to protect the minorities, a special Punjab Boundary Force was established on August 1. However, on September 1 the Boundary Force was abolished because it had surrendered to the 'communal virus'. Thus, the last illusion of the protection of people disappeared. At the same time refugee convoys and trains were attacked. Villages and urban neighbourhoods were burned down all over the Punjab in a spiral of attacks, counter-attacks, retaliation and revenge. It was a case of reciprocal genocide.

The only authority left in the crucial months of August - September, were the various communal leaders. There were instances where communal leaders made attempts to control the violence or where individuals showed great humanity in protecting people belonging to the 'other' community. However, these examples were by far outnumbered by the instances where communal leaders (especially at the district level) actively engaged in aiding and abetting the violence.

Another way of looking at the transition of the violence from 1937-47 is through the number of casualties reported in the fortnightly reports.[471]

---

471. It is important to emphasise the these figures only portrays the number of casualties identified by the British as victims of communal violence.

Graph 1: Development of Violence 1937-1946[472]

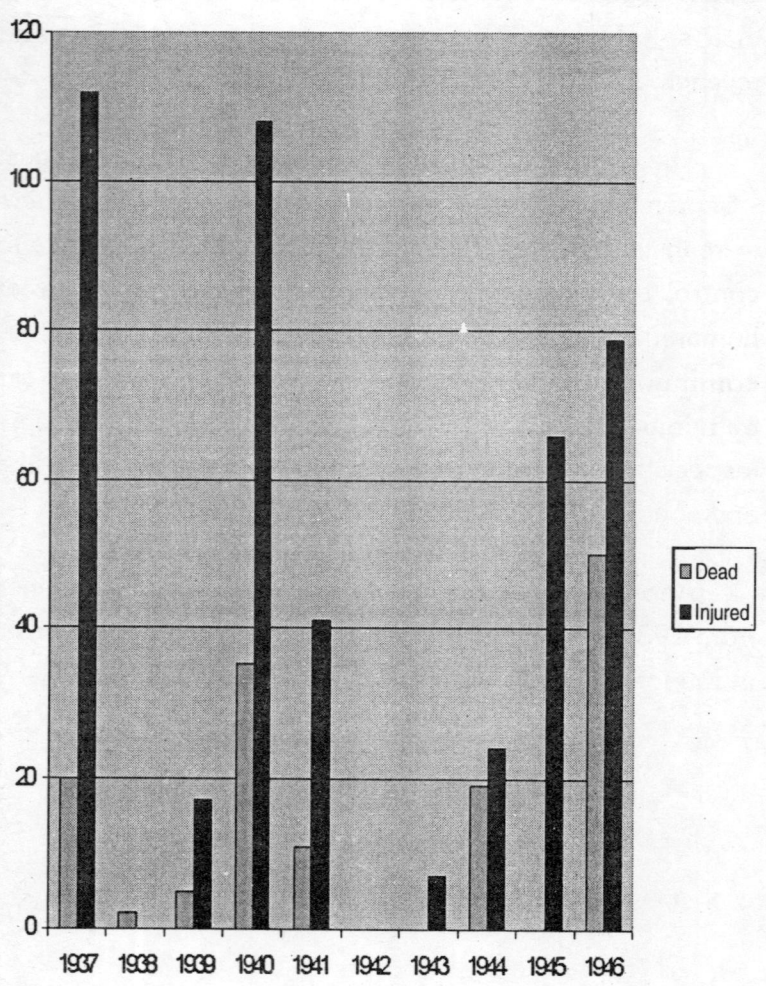

472. Numbers of dead and injured compiled from the fortnightly reports and Governor's letters IOL, L/P&J/5/238-249.

Graph 2: Development of Violence 1937- May 1947[473]

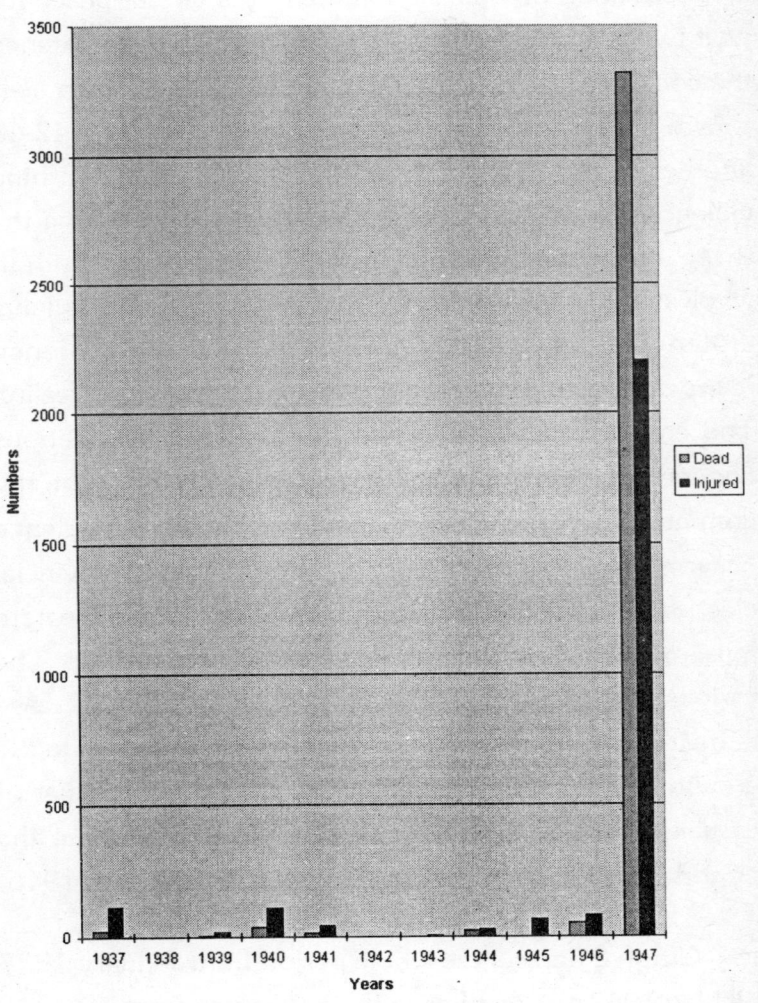

473. Numbers of dead and injured compiled from the fortnightly reports and Governor's letters IOL, L/P&J/5/238-250.

The Graph 1 depicts the development of violence from 1937 to 1946. The provincial elections in 1937 marks the first escalation of violence followed by a virtual peace for next two years. The Lahore resolution in 1940 threatened the coexistence of the three communities once again as is shown by the second escalation in 1940- 41. In 1942-43 another period of uneasy truce prevailed as the diminishing violence was accompanied by growing tension among the three communities. The prospects of direct Indian involvement in World War II, however, kept the communal violence from exploding. In 1944-45 the violence reappeared as the allied victory was fast becoming a reality. The end of war was followed by high-level negotiations concerning the political future of India that kept the communal tension alive. A new escalation in violence occurred in 1946 following the bitterly fought provincial elections. The belligerent election campaign for a separate Muslim state increased the inter-communal hostility. The various private armies also witnessed an alarming increase in their membership and activities, thus contributing to the growth of violent clashes. However, the overall number of casualties was at a rather moderate level throughout the period from 1937-46 with peaks in 1937, 1940 and 1946.

Graph 2 depicts the whole period from January 1937 till May 1947 and testifies to the massive transformation in the violence - from traditional to genocidal violence. The casualties in first five months of 1947 were more than thirteen times higher than the entire numbers compiled from the previous ten years. Furthermore, the graph shows that the number of killed by far exceeded the numbers of injured, which points towards the genocidal intent. The graph, however, only depicts the number of killed and injured until May 1947, as it is impossible to capture the tremendous numbers of casualties that occurred after the announcement of the Partition Plan on June 3 and during partition as such. The enormity of the carnage actually makes it impossible to compile an accurate number of killed and injured. While the lowest estimates place the casualties at 200, 000[474], others place it around 500,000.[475] The recent studies even suggest a figure as high as 800,000.[476] As for the ethnic cleansing, approximately nine million men, women and children were forced into migration, which was roughly one third on the entire Punjabi population.

The second focus in this book has been on the various manifestations of the violence from the provincial elections in 1937 till the partition in August 1947. The communal violence in the Punjab followed more or less a similar pattern from 1937 till 1946, only to assume altogether new forms and proportions. The traditional communal violence had the following features. Firstly, it evolved around the sacrilege of religious places or symbols. Secondly, the participants

---

474. Pendrel Moon, op., cit.
475. G. D. Khosla, op., cit.
476. Urvashi Butalia, op., cit.

were predominantly male. Thirdly, it was considered an urban phenomenon. Fourthly, it mainly occupied public space and lastly, it was bound by prevalent socio- cultural norms.

The forms of violence following the announcement of British withdrawal in February 1947, which was termed 'internecine' by the Governor of Punjab, differed from the traditional violence: Firstly, it was dominated by national discourses and issues of state formation (even though the religious issues continued to be central). Secondly, it spread beyond the urban boundaries to engulf rural areas. Thirdly, it entered the private arena with the attacks on women and children, and lastly, it broke all cultural taboos by inflicting sexual violence on a massive scale. These changes in the violence emphasised the diminishing prospects of a peaceful coexistence. One can thus use the term 'consensual' and 'non-consensual' violence to describe this transition from traditional to genocidal violence. The consensual violence changed into non-consensual when the exchange of violence was transformed from being an act of maintaining tradition into an act of survival. Furthermore, the recipients of the violence were no longer confined by tradition as the fight was now for survival and territory.

The rape and sexual molestation of women during the communal violence played an important part in reinforcing the communal terror. A distinct feature of the partition violence, which set it apart from the earlier riots, was the attack on women. The patriarchal set up made strict delineation between male/public and female/private domain, which is why women were excluded from the public exchange of violence. Therefore, the seriousness of the post 1946 violence was spelt out loud when the women were drawn out of their limited space. Ironically, the same patriarchal belief, which kept them secluded in the four walls, was applied to drag them to the streets. The rape was used as a weapon to conquer the female body as it symbolised the enemy territory.

An important focus of this book has been whether the communal violence was organised. A detailed description of communal conflict in the period 1937 - 47, shows how the violence in Punjab was not merely a spontaneous outburst, but the result of deliberate efforts involving the various private armies; Muslim League National Guard, Rashtriya Swayam Sevak Sangh (RSS) and Akal Fauj. These private armies had originated as defence organisations but symbolised the increasingly militant posture adopted by each community. The military expertise was to some extent provided by professional soldiers who had returned home from World War II. In this connection, one must remember the large-scale recruitment of Punjabis in the British Indian army. Furthermore, the private armies provided a ready-made opportunity for employment, which is also corroborated by the sudden increase in their numbers after 1945. Another pointer to the level of organisation was the use of both crude and sophisticated weapons, ability to make bombs, organise attacks on villages and the well-planned attacks on trains. This also suggested official complicity in transferring information about the movement of refugee trains. The participation of the local police in the riots also points that the official machinery was used to inflict violence on the 'other' community.

The genocidal intent of the violence became fully apparent during the March rioting in Rawalpindi in 1947 because it crossed the threshold between traditional violence and genocidal violence. With this change the aim of the violence was no longer defending one's community, but to ethnically cleanse one's area of the 'other' through mass killings. The unprecedented number of people rendered homeless or forced to take refuge during this period is yet another pointer that the co-existence was no longer considered possible. The violence during actual partition in August 1947 continued these genocidal features but on a massive scale. Hundreds of thousands were killed, tens of thousands were abducted, several thousands raped and more than nine million migrated or roughly one third of the total Punjab populations. This humanitarian catastrophe happened in a short span of four months.

Reciprocal Genocide

Genocide studies has mainly emphasised upon the pivotal role of the state in establishing a case of genocide. That the state-centric approach is inadequate and lopsided is shown in instances like the violence that followed the partition of Punjab, where the state did not have a well-defined role. Despite the absence of state as a perpetrator in Punjab, a reciprocal genocide occurred through organised mass killings that aimed at annihilating the 'Other' community. The violence was not merely spontaneous or a traditional exchange of violence, but was intended to destroy the enemy through actual killings, cutting off of reproductive organs, rapes and dismembering of sexual organs was meant to defile and decimate the future generations. The partition genocide was organised and perpetrated by communal organisations that were aided by the upheavals and turmoil of a state in transition. The partition violence shows that the state need not be the only actor in a genocidal situation. I would, therefore, argue that genocide, and especially a genocidal conflict can also occur when the state is either unwilling or incapable of countering the violence, while the actual power is usurped by various communal groups. Instead of focusing on state involvement per se, the attention should be on processes leading to the genocidal situation.

This study has shown how political changes coupled with a political power vacuum created ample preconditions for a genocidal conflict. In the South Asian context, the phenomenon of communalism needs to be recognised as a structure giving a possible rise to conflicts, which can attain genocidal proportions. In such conflicts the demarcation between the perpetrator and the victim is not clear as in state led and organised genocidal massacres. In the civil-war like situations and inter-ethnic conflicts, the conflicting groups can both be the perpetrators as well as the victims given the control of power by one group vis-à-vis the other in a geographical location. This can be understood in terms of 'reciprocal genocide' where in the absence of a legitimate state or in case of a weak state, two or more non-official power centres emerges to lead and organise the genocidal massacres against each other.

List of Important Persons

(Only people relevant to this book are mentioned below)

- Auchinleck, Sir Claude, Field Marshall, Supreme Commander in India and Pakistan

- Cripps, Sir Stafford, Member of the British war Cabinet. Leader of the Cripps mission to India 1942. Member of the Cabinet Mission to India, 1946.

- Craik, Sir Henry, Governor of Punjab, 1938-41.

- Emerson, Sir Herbert, Governor of Punjab, 1933-38.

- Glancy, Sir Bertrand, Governor of Punjab, 1941-46.

- Jenkins, Sir Evans, Governor of Punjab, 1946-47.

- Jinnah, Muhammad Ali, Leader of the Muslim League. First Governor-General of Pakistan.

- Khan, Khizar Hyat, leader of the Unionist Party and Premier of Punjab, 1943-47.

- Khan, Sir Sikander Hyat, Unionist Party leader. Premier of Punjab, 1937-42.

- Linlithgow, Second Marquis of, Viceroy of India, 1936-43.

- Mountbatten of Burma, First Earl, Viceroy of India 1947. First Governor-General of (independent) India 1947.

- Mudie, Sir Francis, Governor of West Punjab (in Pakistan), 1947.

- Nehru, Jawaharlal, Prominent Congress leader. First Prime Minister of (independent) India.

- Pethick-Lawrence, First Baron, Secretary of State for India 1945-47. Member of the Cabinet Mission to India, 1946.

- Rees, Thomas Wynford, Major General, Commander of Punjab Boundary Force, 1947

- Singh, Baldev, Minister in Punjab 1942-46. Sikh member of the interim Government, 1946-47.

- Singh, Giani Kartar, Sikh leader

- Singh, Tara, Prominent leader of the Akali Sikhs

- Trivedi, Sir C. M., Governor of East Punjab (in India)

- Wavell, Sir Archibald, Viceroy of India, 1943-47.

List of private armies and political parties

(Only those organisations of relevance for this book are mentioned below)

- Akali Dal, Major Sikh Party
- Indian National Congress, Main All India political Party
- Unionist Party, Regional party in the Punjab
- Muslim League, All India Muslim Party
- Jathas, Sikh private armies
- Muslim League National Guards, militant wing of the Muslim League
- Rashtriya Swayamsevak Sangh (*RSS*), militant Hindu volunteer organisation.

Bibliography

Manuscript Sources:

India Office Library and Records, London:

L/P&J (Political and Judicial Records)/5/238-250. (1937-1947)

(These files contains the fortnightly reports from the Punjab Government to the Viceroy and the letter from the Governor of Punjab to the Viceroy)

Printed Sources:

Khosla, G. D. Stern Reckoning: A Survey of the Events Leading Up To and Following The Partition of India, London 1950, (2nd ed., Delhi 1989).

Mansergh, Nicholas and Moon, Penderel, (eds.): Constitutional Relations Between Britain and India: The Transfer of Power 1942-47, [12 Volumes], (TOP) Volume I: The Cripps Mission, January-April 1942; Volume II: 'Quit India', 30 April-21 September 1942; Volume III: Reassertion of Authority, Gandhi's Fast and the Succession To The Viceroyalty, 21 September 1942-12 June 1943; Volume IV: The Bengal Famine and the New Viceroyalty 15 June 1943-31 August 1944; Volume V The Simla Conference: Background and Proceedings September 1944-28 July 1945; Volume VI, The Post-War Phase: New Moves by the Labour Government, 1 August 1945-22 March 1946; Volume VII: The Cabinet Mission, 23 March-29 June 1946; Volume VIII: The Interim Government, 3 July-1 November 1946; Volume IX: The Fixing of a Time Limit, 4 November 1946-22 March 1947; Volume X: The Mountbatten Viceroyalty: Formulation of a Plan, 22 March-30 May 1947; Volume XI: The Mountbatten Viceroyalty: Announcement and reception of the 3rd June Plan, 31 May-7 July 1947; Volume XII: The Mountbatten Viceroyalty: Princes, Partition and Independence, 8 July-15 August 1947, London 1970-83.

Sharma, H.D. (ed.), 100 Best Pre-Independence Speeches, 1870-1947, New Delhi 1998.

Singh, Kirpal (ed.): Select Documents on the Partition of the Punjab 1947: India, India and Pakistan: Punjab Haryana and Himachal Pradesh - India and Punjab - Pakistan, Delhi 1991.

Tirmizi S.A.I. (ed.): The Paradoxes of Partition, vol. 1, New Delhi 1998

Secondary Sources

Books:

Aiyar, Swarma: Violence and the State in the Partition of Punjab, Cambridge 1994 (PhD dissertation).

Andreopoulos, George J. (ed.): Genocide: Conceptual and Historical Dimensions, University of Pennsylvania Press, 1994.

Bauman, Zygmunt: Modernity and the Holocaust, Oxford 1989.

Basu, Tapan, et al.: Khaki Shorts and Saffron Flags: A Critique of the Hindu Right, New Delhi 1993.

Brass, Paul R.: Language, Religion and Politics in North India, Cambridge University Press 1974.

Butalia, Urvashi: The Other Side of Silence. Voices from the Partition of India, Delhi 1998.

Chalk, Frank and Kurt Jonassohn: The History and Sociology of Genocide. Analyses and Case Studies, Yale University Press 1990.

Chandra, Bipan: Communalism in Modern India, New Delhi 1984.

Chandra, Bipan et al: India's Struggle for Independence 1857-1947, New Delhi 1988.

Charny, Israel (ed.): Genocide. A Critical Bibliographic Review, London 1988.

Das, Suranjan: Communal Violence in Bengal 1905-1947, Delhi 1991.

Das, Veena (ed.): Mirrors of Violence: Communities, Riots and Survivors in South Asia, New Delhi 1990.

Dobkowski, Michael & Isodor Wallimann (eds.): Genocide and the Modern Age, New York 1987.

Drost, Pieter N: Genocide, Leyden 1959.

Engineer, Asghar Ali: Communalism and communal Violence in India. An Analytical approach to the Hindu-Muslim Conflict, Delhi 1991.

Fein, Helen: Genocide - A Sociological Perspective, 1990.

Freitag, Sandria: Collective action and Community: Public Arenas and the emergence of Communalism in North India, California 1989.

Gilmartin, David: Empire and Islam: Punjab and the Making of Pakistan, London 1988.

Golwarkar, M. S. : We, or our Nationhood defined, Delhi 1939.

Hasan, Mushirul (ed.): India's Partition: Process, Strategy and Mobilisation. Delhi 1993.

Hasan, Mushirul (ed.): Inventing Boundaries. Gender, Politics and the Partition of India, Oxford University Press New Delhi, 2000.

Horowitz, Irving Louis: State, Power and Mass Murder, 1976.

Jalal, Ayesha: The Sole Spokesman: Jinnah, The Muslim League and the Demand for Pakistan, Cambridge 1985.

Jaffrelot, Christophe: The Hindu Nationalist Movement and Indian Politics: 1925 to the 1990's, Penguin Books India 1999.

Kakar, Sudhir: The Colour of Violence, Penguin 1996.

Kaul, Suvir (ed.): The Partition of Memory. The Aftermath of the Division of India", New Delhi 2001.

Kuper, Leo: Genocide. Its Political Use in the Twentieth Century, Yale University Press 1981.

Lemkin, Raphael: Aixs Rule in Occupied Europe, Washington 1944.

Low, D. A. & Howard Brasted (eds.): Freedom, Trauma, Continuities. Northern India and Independence, Delhi 1998.

Low, D A.: Britain and Indian Nationalism. The Imprint of Ambiguity 1929-1942,

Melson, Robert: Revolution and Genocide. The Origins of the Armenian Genocide and the Holocaust, 1992.

Menon, Ritu & Kamla Bhasin: Borders and Boundaries: Women in India's Partition, New Delhi 1998.

Moon, Penderel: Divide and Quit, London 1961.

Pandey, Gyanendra: The Construction of Communalism in Colonial North India, Delhi 1990.

Panikkar, K. N. (ed.): Communalism in India: History, Politics and Culture, Delhi 1991.

Prasad, Bimal: Pathway to India's Partition, vol. 1, The Foundations of Muslim Nationalism, Delhi 1999.

Prasad, Bimal: Pathway to India's Partition, vol. 2, A Nation within a Nation, 1877-1937, Delhi 2000.

Robinson, Francis: Separatism Among Indian Muslims: The Politics of the United Provinces Muslims 1880-1923, Cambridge 1974.

Rudé, George: The Crowd in History: A Study of Popular Disturbances in France and England, 1730-1848, New York 1964.

Rummel, R.J.: Death by Government, New Brunswick, 1994.

Salim, Ahmad (ed.): Lahore 1947, India Research Press New Delhi, 2001.

Sarkar, Sumit: Modern India 1885-1947, New Delhi 1983.

Sidhwa, Bapsi: Ice Candy Man, Penguin Books 1989.

Singh, Anita Inder: The Origins of the Partition of India, 1936-1947, Delhi 1987.

Singh, Kirpal: Partition of Punjab, Patiala 1972.

Spear, Percival: History of India, vol. II, New Delhi, 1978.

Staub, Ervin: The Root of Evil, 1989.

Symonds, Richards: In the Margins of Independence. A Relief Worker in India and Pakistan, 1942 – 1949, Oxford University Press Karachi, 2001.

Talbot, Ian: Freedom's Cry: The Popular Dimension in the Pakistan Movement and Partition Experience in North-West India, Karachi 1996.

Talbot, Ian: Khizr Tiwana: The Punjab Unionist Party and Partition of India, London 1996.

Talbot, Ian: Provincial Politics and the Pakistan Movement: The Growth of the Muslim League in North-West and North-East India 1937-47, Karachi 1988.

Talbot, Ian: Punjab and the Raj 1849-1947, New Delhi 1988.

Talbot, Ian & Gurharpal Singh (eds.): Region and Partition. Bengal, Punjab and the Partition of the Subcontinent", Karachi 1999.

Thapar, Romilla: The History of India, vol. I, New Delhi, 1987.

Tucker, Sir Francis: While Memory Serves, London 1950.

Whitaker, B: Report on the Question of the Prevention and Punishment of the Crime of Genocide, United Nations Economic and Social Council, 1985.

Wolpert, Stanley: Gandhi's Passion. The Life and Legacy of Mahatma Gandhi, Oxford University Press New York, 2001.

Wolpert, Stanley: Jinnah of Pakistan, Oxford University Press New York, 1984.

Yong, Tan Tai & Gyanesh Kudaisya: The Aftermath of Partition in South Asia, London 2000.

Articles

Ahmed, Ishtiaq: "The 1947 Partition of Punjab: Arguments put Forth before the Punjab Boundary Commission by the Parties involved", in Ian Talbot and Gurharpal Singh (eds.): Region and Partition. Bengal, Punjab and the Partition of the Subcontinent", Karachi 1999.

Aiyar, Swarna: "August Anarchy: The Partition Massacres in Punjab, 1947", in D.A. Low & Howard Brasted (eds.): Freedom, Trauma, Continuities. Northern India and Independence, Delhi 1998.

Amiruddin, Mian: "Memories of Partition", in Ahmad Salim (ed.), Lahore 1947, India Research Press Delhi, 2001.

Andropoulos, George J: "Introdoction: The Calculus of Genocide", in George J. Andreopoulos (ed.): Genocide: Conceptual and Historical Dimensions, University of Pennsylvania Press, 1994.

Ansari, Sarah: "Pakistan, Partition and Gender: Fashioning the Shape of Pakistani Womanhood", in International Journal of Punjab Studies, vol. 6, no. 1, 1999, pp. 17-32.

Brass, Paul R.: "A Reply to Francis Robinson", Journal of Commonwealth and Comparative Politics, 15, 3 (1977), p. 231-234.

Butalia, Urvashi: "Community, State and Gender: On Women's Agency during Partition", Economic and Political Weekly, Vol. XXVIII, no. 17, 24th April 1993.

Charny, Israel: "Towards a Generic Definition of Genocide" in George J. Andreopoulos (ed.): Genocide: Conceptual and Historical Dimensions, University of Pennsylvania Press, 1994.

Copland, Ian: "The Further Shores of Partition: Ethnic Cleansing in Rajastan 1947", Past and Present, No. 160, August 1998, pp. 203-239.

Dadrian, Vahakn: "A Typology of Genocide", in International Review of Modern Sociology 5, 1975.

Das, Veena: "Introduction", in Veena Das(ed.): Mirrors of Violence: Communities, Riots and Survivors in South Asia, New Delhi 1990.

Das, Veena & Ashis Nandy: "Violence, Victimhood and the Language of Silence", in Veena Das (ed.): The Word and the World: Fantasy, Symbol and Record, New Delhi 1983.

Datta, V.N.: "Panjabi Refugees and the Urban Development of Greater Delhi", in Mushirul Hasan (ed.): Inventing Boundaries. Gender, Politics and the Partition of India, Oxford University Press New Delhi, 2000.

Fein, Helen: "Accounting for Genocide after 1945: Theories and some Findings", International Journal on Group Rights, 1, 1993, pp. 79-106.

Fein, Helen: "Genocide, Terror, Life integrity and War Crimes" in George J. Andreopoulos (ed.): Genocide: Conceptual and Historical Dimensions, University of Pennsylvania Press, 1994.

Fein, Helen: "Scenarios of Genocide: Models of Genocide and Critical responses"; in I.W. Charny (ed.) 1984, Toward the Understanding and Prevention of Genocide: Proceedings of the International Conference on the Holocaust and Genocide, Boulder/London, 1984.

Francisco, Jason: "In the Heat of Fratricide. The literature of India's Partition Burning Freshly", in Mushirul Hasan (ed.): Inventing Boundaries. Gender, Politics and the Partition of India, Oxford University Press New Delhi, 2000.

Gilmartin, David: "Religious Leadership and the Pakistan Movement in the Punjab", Modern Asian Studies, 13, 3 (1979), pp. 485-517.

Glick, Leonard B: "Religion and Genocide", in Israel Charny: The Widening Circle of Genocide, 1994.

Hansen, Anders Bjørn: "Folkemordsforskningen gennem 50 år – En definitorisk tilgang" in: Den Jyske Historiker, nr. 90 (Folkemord), december 2000, pp. 39-59.

Harff, Barbara: "The Etiology of Genocides", in Isidor Wallimann & Michael N. Dobkowski (eds.): Genocide and the Modern Age. Etiology and Case Studies of Mass Death, New York 1987.

Harff, Barbara & Ted Robert Gurr: "Towards Emperical Theory of Genocides and Politicides: Identification and Measurement of Cases since 1945", International Studies Quarterly, (1988) 32, pp. 359-371.

Harris, Ruth: "The 'Child of the Barbarian'; Rape, Race and Nationalism in France during the First World War", Past and Present, 141, (Nov. 1993) pp. 170-206.

Hasan, Mushirul: "Introduction", in Mushirul Hasan (ed.): India's Partition: Process, Strategy and Mobilisation. Delhi 1993.

Hasan, Mushirul: "Prologue", in Mushirul Hasan (ed.): Inventing Boundaries. Gender, Politics and the Partition of India, Oxford University Press New Delhi, 2000.

Hasan, Mushirul: "The Muslim Mass Contacts Campaign. Analysis of a strategy of Political Mobilization", in Mushirul Hasan (ed.): India's Partition: Process, Strategy and Mobilisation. Delhi 1993.

Huttenbach, Henry R.: "Introduction", Journal of Genocide Research vol. 1, 1999.

Huttenbach, Henry R: "Locating the Holocaust on the Genocide Spectrum: Towards a Methodology of definition and Categorization", Holocaust and Genocide Studies, vol. 3, no. 3, 1988.

Jalal, Ayesha: "Exploding Communalism: The Politics of Muslim Identity in South Asia", in Sugata Bose & Ayesha Jalal (eds.): Nationalism, Democracy & Development. State and Politics in India, Delhi 1998.

Jalal, Ayesha: "Secularism, Subalterns and the Stigma of 'Communalism': Partition Historiography revisited", Modern Asian Studies, 3o, 3 (1996) pp. 681-689.

Kaul, Suvir (ed.): "Introduction", in The Partition of Memory. The Aftermath of the Division of India", New Delhi 2001.

Levene, Mark: "Creating a Modern 'Zone of Genocide': The Impact of Nation and State Formation on Eastern Anatolia, 1878-1923", Holocaust and Genocide Studies, vol. 12 no. 3, 1998.

Levene, Mark: "Is the Holocaust Simply Another Example of Genocide?", Patterns of Prejudice, vol. 28, no. 2, 1994.

Malik, Iftikhar, H.: "Identity Formation and Muslim Party Politics in the Punjab, 1897-1936: A Retrospective Analysis", Modern Asian Studies, 29, 2 (1995), pp. 293-323.

Markusen, Eric : "What is Genocide? A Search for Answers" in Steven L. B. Jensen (ed.): Genocide: Cases, Comparisons and Contemporary Debates, forthcoming 2002.

Mayaram, Shail: "Speech, Silence and the Making of Partition Violence in Mewat", Shahid Amin (ed.): Subaltern Studies IX. Writings on South Asian History and society, New Delhi 1997.

Menon, Ritu & Kamla Bhasin: "Recovery, Rupture, Resistance: Indian State and Abduction of Women during Partition", Economic and Political Weekly, Vol. XXVIII, no. 17, 24th April 1993.

Moore, R.J: "Jinnah and the Pakistan Demand", Modern Asian Studies, 17, 4, (1983) pp. 529-561.

Nanda, B. R. : "Nehru, the Indian National Congress and the Partition of India, 1935-47", in C. H. Philips & M. D. Wainwright (eds.): The Partition of India, Policies and perspectives, 1935-47, London 1971.

Pandey, Gyanendra: "The Colonial Construction of 'Communalism': British Writing on Banaras in the Nineteenth Century", Ranajit Guha (ed.): Subaltern Studies VI. Writings on South Asian History and Society, New Delhi 1989.

Pandey, Gyanendra: "The Prose of Otherness", David Arnold (ed.): Subaltern Studies VIII. Essays in Honour of Ranajit Guha, New Delhi 1994.

Robinson, Francis: "Nation Formation: The Brass Thesis and Muslim separatism", Journal of Commonwealth and Comparative Politics, 15, 3 (1977) pp. 215-230.

Robinson, Francis: "Reviews of Stanley Wolpert: Jinnah of Pakistan, New York 1984, & Ayesha Jalal: The Sole Spokesman: Jinnah, The Muslim League and the Demand for Pakistan, Cambridge 1985, Modern Asian Studies, 20, 3 (1986), pp. 611-618.

Roy, Asim: "The High Politics of India's Partition. The Revisionist Perspective", Modern Asian Studies, 24, 2, (1990), pp. 385-415

Samad, Yunas: "Reflections on Partition: Pakistan Perspective", International journal of Punjab Studies, 4, 1 (1997) pp. 43-61.

Snyder, David & Charles Tilly: "Hardship and Collective Violence in France 1830 - 1960", American Sociological Review, 1972.

Talbot, Ian: "British Rule in Punjab 1849-1947: Characteristics and Consequences", Journal of Imperial and Commonwealth History, 19, 2, (1991), pp. 203-221.

Talbot, Ian: "Literature and the Human Drama of the 1947 Partition", in: D.A. Low & Howard Brasted (eds.) Freedom, Trauma, Continuities. Northern India and Independence, Delhi 1998.

Talbot, Ian: "The Growth of the Muslim League in the Punjab, 1937-1946", Journal of Commonwealth and Comparative Politics, 20, 1, (1982), pp. 5-24.

Talbot, Ian: "The Role of the Crowd in the Muslim League Struggle for Pakistan", Journal of Imperial and Commonwealth History, vol. 21, 2 (1993), pp. 307-333.

Thompson, E. P: "The Moral Economy of the English Crowd in Eighteenth Century," Past and Present, 50 (1971).

Wasseem, Mohammad: "Partition, Migration and Assimilation: A Comparative Study of Pakistani Punjab", International journal of Punjab Studies, 4, 1 (1997) pp. 21-41.

Willner, David: "Women as Participants in the Pakistan Movement: Modernization and the Promise of a Morale State", Modern Asian Studies, 30, 3 (1996) pp. 573-590.

Yong, Tan Tai: "Prelude to Partition: Sikh Responses to the Demand for Pakistan", International journal of Punjab Studies, 1, 2 (1994), pp. 167-195.

Yong, Tan Tai: "Sir Cyril Goes to India: Partition, Boundary-Making and Disruptions in the Punjab", International journal of Punjab Studies, 4, 1 (1997) pp. 1-20.

NOTES

NOTES

About India Research Press

India Research Press is a collectively run book publisher with support of Authors and Editors. Since our founding in 1999, we have tried to meet the needs of readers who are exploring, or are committed to the politics of change.

Our goal is to publish books that encourage critical thinking and constructive action on the key political, cultural, social, economic and ecological issues shaping life in the Indian Sub-continent and in the world.

In this way, we hope to give expression to a wide diversity of democratic and social movements.

India Research Press publishes Original works-as well as-works under Rights with various University and Academic publishers throughout the world.

The Group now has twenty two titles to its credit and another six, scheduled for the next few months.

Since our conception, we have added two new imprints to our existing line of Academic publishing.

The group is proud to introduce its three divisions of publishing....

India Research Press
Academic publishing division.

Swankit
General division – Health, Non Fiction and Educational titles.

Tara
General division – Mass Market including Fiction.

The group is headed by Anuj Bahri Malhotra, its CEO & Commissioning Manager. He is assisted by an efficient and professional staff of Editors, Administrator and Office Assistants. Born to a bookseller's family, running the most sought after bookshop in the country, Anuj has a long inherited experience in the Indian Book Industry.

Our List of Titles

- Divided Kashmir : Old Problems, New Opportunities for India, Pakistan and the Kashmiri People.
  By: Mushtaqur Rahman

- British Conquest and Dominion of India : Two volume set.
  By: Sir Penderal Moon

- India and the Bomb : Public Opinion and Nuclear Options.
  By: David Courtright & Amitabh Mattoo

- Rural Labour Relations in India.
  By: T.J.Byres & Karin Kapadia

- Architecture of Indian Desert: [Illus in Colour & B/W]
  By: Kulbhushan & Minakshi Jain

- Central Asia : A travelers companion.
  By: Katherine Hopkirk [distribution only]

- Rogue States : The Rule of Force in World Affairs.
  By: Noam Chomsky

- Stolen Harvest : The Hijacking of the Global Food Supply.
  By: Vandana Shiva

- Heaven's Child and other Poems
  By: Sameer Kak

- Natural Resource Management and Institutional Change.
  An ODI/IRP joint series.
  By: Diana Carney and John Farrington

- Development as process. An ODI/IRP joint series.
  By: David Mosse, John Farrington and Alan Rew.

- Quiz Master India. Volume 1
  By: Sanjay Sharma

- Quiz Master India. Volume 2
  By: Sanjay Sharma

- ....and the answer is a pineapple
  By: Claudia Hyles

- Lahore 1947 : The last days of Lahore at Partition
  By: Ahmed Salim., Intro by : Ian Talbot

- Democracy-a failure, Shefocracy-the solution, for human welfare.
  By: Dr. Rabin Mukherjee

- India-Sri Lanka relations and Sri Lanka's Ethnic Conflict Documents : 1947-2000. [set of 5 volumes]
  By: Dr. Avtar Singh Bhasin

- Security in the New Millenium : Views from South Asia
  By: Rajesh M. Basrur

- The Saffron Book : A study of the Saffron politics.
  By: Prafull Goradia

- Roots of Rhetoric : Politics of Nuclear Weapons in India & Pakistan
  By: Haider K. Nizamani

- Democracy and Dictatorship in South Asia : Dominant Classes and Political Outcomes in India, Pakistan and Bangladesh
  By: Robert W. Stern

- Quiz Master India : A Student's guide to Success [omnibus]
  By: Sanjay Sharma.

Our Forthcoming Titles

- Rewriting Indian History
  By : Francois Gautier

- Katha Sagar : A collection of Prem Chand's Stories
  By: R. Gupta

- Hanklyn-Janklin : A rumble-tumble of Indian Words
  used in everyday English.
  By: Nigel Hankin

- The Sustainable Livelihood Series :
  An ODI/IRP joint series
  Volume One /Volume Two /Volume Three ....[continuing series]

- Pakistan : In the Face of the Afghan Conflict 1979-1985
  By : Frédéric Grare

****

For further information, write to........

India Research Press
Publishers
B 4 / 22 Safdarjung Enclave, New Delhi – 110029. India
Tel : 619 6234, Telefax : 461 8637. e mail : bahrisons@vsnl.com

India
Research   **SwanKit**   **Tara Press**
Press

216